So let the artists do it.

DISTANZ

Conversations with ten artists from the Sammlung Hoffmann

and

ERIKA HOFFMANN-KOENIGE

the collector who let them

Edited by
ISABEL PARKES

So let the artists do it documents a collection of contemporary art through a series of relationships between artist and patron, a historically essential but underexplored link. Erika Hoffmann-Koenige's recollections about her and her late husband's encounters with artists and their work frame the situations that catalyzed many of their earliest acquisitions and a number of the experiences that lead them to create a space for the public to engage with art in their Berlin home. Conversations between curator Isabel Parkes and ten artists from the collection follow, offering insight into specific works and processes, as well as the contexts and ideals that informed what is today considered one of Germany's most significant collections of contemporary art.

What emerges from this combination of voices is a prismatic reflection of the ever-changing conditions in which contemporary art is created and experienced. During the past fifty years in which the Hoffmanns have collected art, a market has become an industry, single works have become trademarks, and their once-unknown makers, household names. Artists today are equal parts moral guide and celebrity, called upon to navigate their roles with savvy and grace. Patrons are more known for naming museum wings than facilitating careers.

The following conversations illuminate a different configuration, defined by a tight interconnection of public and private, life and art. Through a combination of narrative styles and lines of questioning, these texts foreground symmetry and synergy between individuals, and explore a handful of vital themes of art-making—among them fantasy, memory, and surprise. They attempt to treat the personal and political with equal weight and, in the spirit of the Sammlung Hoffmann, rely on the strength of distinct voices in order to create a new whole. This publication, the first to emphasize Erika Hoffmann-Koenige's role, also coincides with the donation of the Sammlung Hoffmann to the State Museums of Dresden, perhaps her clearest statement yet about the purpose and place of art. *Berlin, 2021*

MONICA BONVICINI

Monica Bonvicini really made an impression on me and Rolf with how she critiqued downright tragic, bad behavior through grotesque modes of expression. I thought her video *Hausfrau Swinging* (1997) was simply wild. This is of course not to mention its finesse—her use of slow motion, repetition, and sounds that make you flinch. The idea of a woman in a blind fury, with a cardboard house on her head, running into a wall over and over again spoke to me directly. It was only later that I recognized the inspiration came from Louise Bourgeois's *Femme Maison* (1946–47). Today it is practically impossible to imagine that art made by women did not have an audience for so long. I always found it intriguing that female artists expressed themselves differently than male ones. I was never particularly interested in feminism; it was the different sensibility that interested me.

Before Rolf and I moved to Berlin, when we were involved in the Friends' Association of the Museum Abteiberg in Mönchengladbach and the Gesellschaft für Moderne Kunst (Society for Modern Art) in Cologne, it went entirely unquestioned that men—and white men of course—were the ones who almost exclusively had exhibitions. Women were obviously also active at the time, but their work was hardly ever shown. Johannes Cladders drew a lot of inspiration from his meetings with Konrad Fischer. Both of them belonged to a clique that called the shots. I have since read that artists like Donald Judd and Dan Flavin even went as far as to threaten a gallerist who represented them by saying things like, "If you work with her, if you show her, we're gone." When I read that, I could even more so imagine the rage that led to the so-called radical attitudes of artists like Carolee Schneemann, Charlotte Moorman, and Lynda Benglis. No one looked at their work. This is what Nancy Spero told me, too. Everyone visited her husband, Leon Golub, but no one wanted to peek in her studio, which was just next to his. If you experience this, decade after decade, then of course an anger builds up that lasts generations. With these anecdotes in mind, I am fully able to comprehend Monica's critique of institutions and her use of provocation as principle. Both are part of a critique of the world as she finds it and cannot bear. But what I also like is that she wants to entertain. Still today, it frequently surprises me how little this aspect is taken into consideration by those who see only her work in terms of its aggression. Of course, she wants to be provocative and to elicit a reaction. This can be read as rejection—it's often meant to. But it's also supposed to make you think, because that's what it all comes down to for Monica. *As told to Isabel Parkes*

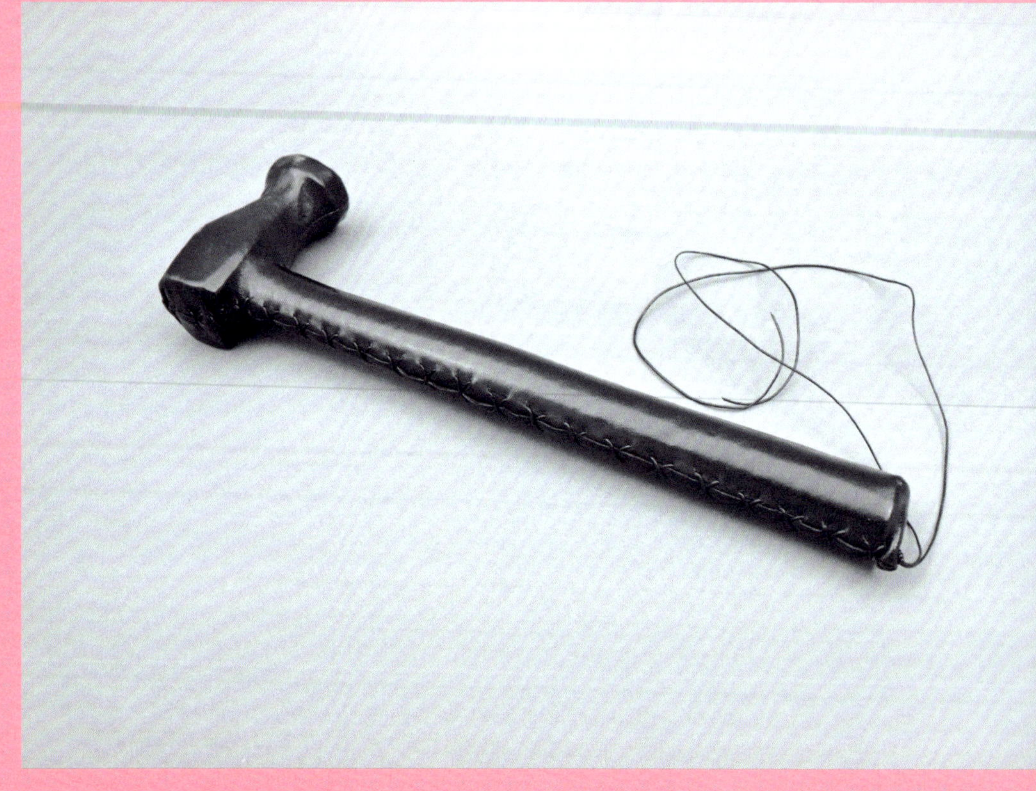

Leather Hammer #1, 2004

What are you working on at the moment?

I drew a lot this spring and came to the studio almost every day through an empty city. During most of the first lockdown in Berlin, only my studio manager and I were here, so I just started drawing and then I couldn't stop!

I'm currently working on a show in Bielefeld with various new works, including a video that is quite simple and dense: making it almost happened by chance, as I biked to the studio while filming with my cell phone from inside my back pocket. What developed from these shoots is an abstract landscape of colors and flesh. Birds provide a soundtrack because of the season, as do cars, although initially there was little traffic. The sound produced by my body as I pedal is constant and rhythmic, almost like a heart beating or blood pumping. It's called *I See a White Building, Pink and Blue* (2020), which refers to a story by Oliver Sacks about a blind lady who experienced hallucinations. The video explores the idea of wanting to see and needing clarity at a time when precisely that is impossible.

Architecture has long been central to your practice. What kind of space will the video be shown in?

In the Kunsthalle Bielefeld, which was designed by Phillip Johnson. During my research for the exhibition, I discovered that Johnson once hosted an evening at the Glass House during which John Cage presented a piece made from the sounds of cars—windshield wipers, doors slamming—and the Velvet Underground came and drove a Cadillac directly into the garden. Phillip Johnson and the Velvet Underground didn't fit together in my mind and I liked that dissonance. Initially, I thought about combining the Velvet Underground's music with Johnson's ideas about transparency, but the video ended up being the opposite: about not seeing anything.

Your *Leather Hammer #1* (2004) is presently installed in the Residenzschloss in Dresden, the opposite of a modern setting. What do you make of that?

I love it. The exhibition title there is great, *Monica Bonvicini and the tools of Elector August of Saxony*, although I never thought my hammer would end up alongside the collection of a king!

Your work is often positioned in terms of the idea of destruction, but placing the hammer next to other tools moves us more towards a vocabulary of construction.

This is part of what I like. For me, the work is also about caring for simple tools. When I say "caring" I mean respecting and preserving beautiful objects. I think of simple tools that are required to build things, and of making them into objects of desire. Desire doesn't age. It is inscribed in crafts and beauty and in history as a value. I love that this piece sits alongside royal hammers.

What do you mean when you say desire here?

It's always impossible to define because it's a concept that changes fluidly and relies on context. I think my work *DESIRE* (2006), which was installed on the roof of a mall in Pasadena in California, captures what I mean. There I added "DESIRE" among shops' logos that adorned a façade. For the invitation, I removed the logos as a way to emphasize the building's white, monolithic architecture. "Desire" could have been read with the other logos, but at the same time, negated itself, because the work's mirrored surface practically disappeared against the very blue sky it reflected. I think that's what desire is: massive, loud and clear wanting, and at the same time, the negation of it. In that sense, desire is a form of fetish, and you can apply it to Marxist theory, capitalism, museums, and so on.

We're trained to desire all the time.

Right, but personally, I don't think I desire many things.

Does desire play a role when you're making work?

Yes and no. I always have to change everything I see in front of me, and I like to create new realities with my installations and sculptures. So yes, I feel a desire for change.

Often your work gets couched in terms of toughness and aggression. Do you also understand it in those terms?

After many years, I better understand why people say that. For a long time, I really didn't. I personally still do not see my work as aggressive. What is aggressive work? Equally well, I don't know what to say when my work is described in terms of delicacy or femininity.

How do you shift between languages—English, Italian, German—in your practice?

I have fun with them! Recently, I was thinking something that made me laugh out loud and only later realized it was half-English and half-German. To be able to speak and understand different languages offers a doorway to different cultures and ways of thinking. I have also always found translation

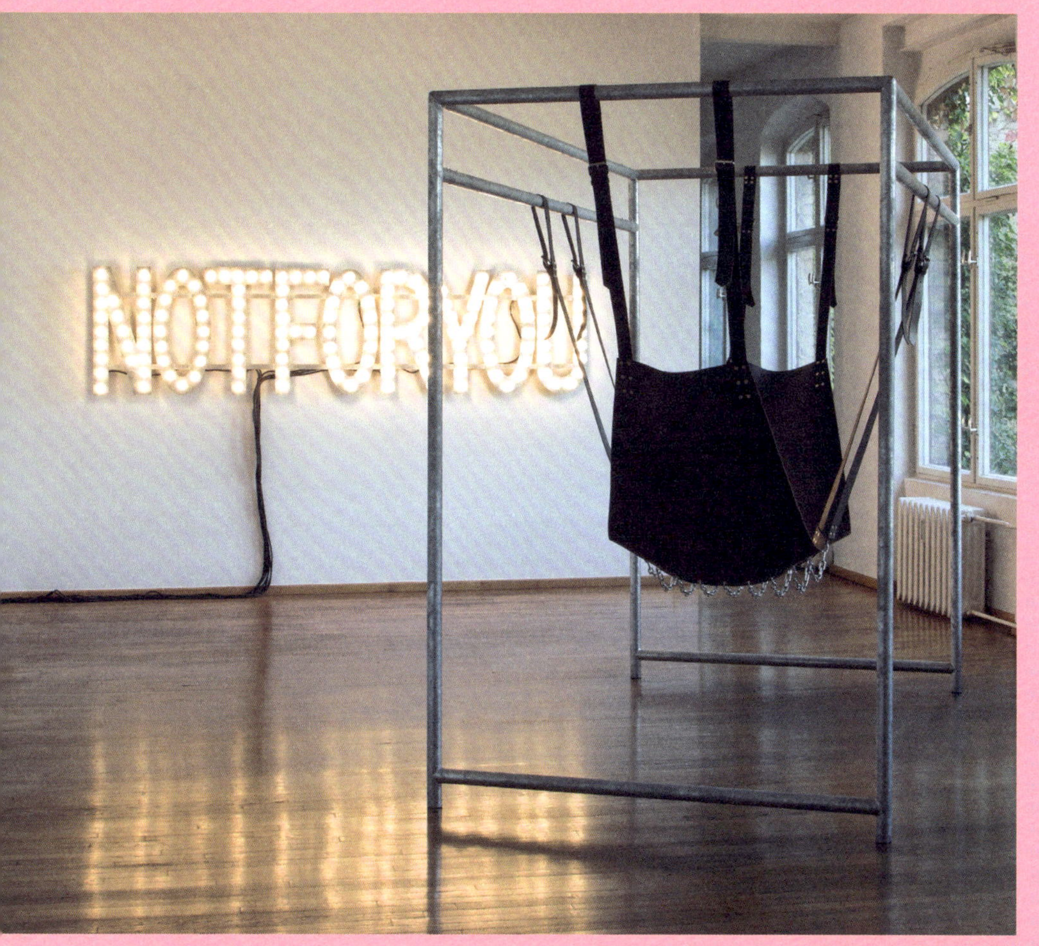

NOT FOR YOU, 2006
Pavilion, 2002
Sammlung Hoffmann Installation XX, 2016–17

interesting and think that to translate is to both create and disrupt. There is a certain violence to it.

At the same time, languages are something inherently personal. I still today do not use certain words in German because I do not feel comfortable with them. I guess it's also a question of style. I learned foreign languages by using dictionaries and still have a small collection. Back in the day, there was no Google Translate. Language used to seem much stiffer and more serious than it does now. The words in the dictionary felt almost religious, practically carrying forth some sort of truth.

Of course, in violence, in search of truth, one finds performance. There are turning pages, for example in Lyotard, Derrida, Butler, and Preciado. There are questions of identities, systems, and quotations that interrupt how we read a page. Language is an imperative, and I think you find that in works of mine like *NOT FOR YOU* (2006), *RUN* (2012), and *SATISFYME* (2010). It's not by chance that artists like Barbara Kruger or Jenny Holzer work with language in such a powerful and public way. This use of language is for me about defining a politics rooted in traditions of masculinity and by this point, everyone has had enough of that.

Having been working now for thirty years, you're squarely in a stage of your career in which you're being told what your work is or is not about. I imagine there are many times where you don't agree with what you hear, but I also think questions of interpretation are interesting.

I do too. Definitely growing up as an artist in the nineties and 2000s, my relationship to the paradox of finding and being given meaning feels complex. I'm happy that people think they know what I do, because it means my work lands with them. At the same time, it bothers me, because it puts me in a drawer, and I don't want that—nobody does. In the nineties, at least in Germany, I was in quite a singular position, working with a strong sculptural language to address themes like sexuality and architecture. If people found my installation *Wallfuckin'* (1995–96) shocking back then, I can only laugh now, because it is nothing compared to what they will see today.

Another element of interpretation is that being a female artist has been and remains tough. Being a foreigner has been tough at times, as well. No matter where I have lived, I have not belonged. One has to both adapt and strike back, and the strike is really against ghosts, against things one cannot see immediately.

Has that changed for you in today's more globalized, digital world or through collective movements like #MeToo?

The idea of openly supporting each other as happens today on social media did not used to exist. Even a few years ago, people, and I mean specifically my students, didn't want to talk about feminism. When I was young, I thought my and others' efforts could be enough to change the way that women are seen, in particular in the art world. Of course, a lot has changed, but it is still not enough. Some people regard me as a difficult woman, and I have to admit, it's never a label I thought I would have.

Who were the difficult women when you were younger?

Everybody!

I think today the difficult woman is also a marketed asset. Do you think that changing galleries has repositioned you in relation to this idea?

One projects the notion being difficult by changing galleries. But more so, at least on my end, the change concerned another naïve notion, which was that we—me and the gallery, me and the curator—were doing something together.

Can you tell me about your relationship with Erika Hoffmann?

Erika is one of the few collectors who really collects my work in an ongoing way. Not only that, but she's in dialogue with me even when it comes to the smallest details, for example how to install a wall as part of a piece. This shows a respect towards both art and artist that I do not take for granted. I also love the way she opened up her collection and life to Berliners at a time where there were really no collectors here. There is a lot to be learned from how she works. Erika also continues to surprise me, for example when she installed *NOT FOR YOU* (2006) in the waiting room of her collection. She blinded visitors with it as they entered, offering a physical reminder that art is not always easy and that they were not necessarily in an easy place.

Tell me about winning the Preis der Neue Nationalgalerie in 2005.

What do you want to hear? That year we managed to change the structure of the prize by getting an actual budget to produce new work. At the time, this was very important, because I felt strongly that a museum should support young artists beyond just giving them space.

I initially planned to have a large sculpture: a space defined by glass walls. Unfortunately, the production of it was challenging and the budget insufficient, so instead I developed an installation called *Never Again* (2005). The work is essentially a scaffolding structure holding up twelve love swings, which I designed. The design negates the function while still allowing viewers to engage the swings, which are hung with chains from the scaffolding, as objects of fantasy or fetish. The installation was by turns very quiet and extremely loud when viewers used the swings. I like to think of the work as one that literally opened up the museal experience for people. I understood winning the prize as a thanks from the city of Berlin, for which I like to think I did a lot back in the day. Berlin does not say thank you easily or really ever, actually, so this remains a special moment in my relationship with the city.

Let's return to your recent drawings.

Before lockdown, I had never found time to make as many as I did recently. I used stencil lettering, which is a pretty laborious process. The drawings appear in the Bielefeld show, *Lover's Material* (2020), which comes from a phrase used to describe one of Phillip Johnson's lovers. I thought it was patronizing, but also quite of its time. I can't imagine that today anyone would write this about a gay man. At the same time, I feel it aptly describes the way relationships can sometimes be between lovers, as well as between artists and institutions.

The phrase reminds me of when people tell women that they "love their enthusiasm."

Yes! Normally, this phrase would be wielded at a woman, but here, it's used to describe a man. I've been rereading Roland Barthes' *Lover's Discourse: Fragments*, alongside texts about feminist anger and language by Natalie Diaz, Soraya Chemaly and Andrea Dworkin. I'm incorporating and editing quotations as I find them as part of the ongoing search for new narratives.

KATHARINA GROSSE

I first noticed one of Katharina Grosse's sprayed works at the exhibition *Selections Fall 1999* at the Drawing Center in New York. Something dark green and black was spreading out between the ceiling and two walls, almost like moss, mold, or mildew. It was with this first impression that I suggested Katharina Grosse for the Preis der Nationalgalerie in 2000. Every year, members of the Friends' Association are invited to nominate artists. Katharina made the shortlist along with Olafur Eliasson, Christian Jankowski, and Dirk Skreber. The four of them worked alongside one another in the main hall of the Hamburger Bahnhof in Berlin, in the middle of which Katharina built a powerful, wedge-shaped wall which she spray-painted colorfully. It must have been too unusual for the jury, because Skreber ended up winning the prize.

Rolf—who initiated the prize when we were members of the board of trustees of the Freunde der Nationalgalerie (Friends of the National Gallery)—got to know Katharina while she was constructing her work. He became the *de facto* curator of this first exhibition, as nobody at the Hamburger Bahnhof seemed to feel responsible for it. Rolf, Katharina, and I then began to think about what she could do with us at home, but it wasn't immediately clear to either Rolf or me how her work could fit with our concept, which involved changing our set-up every year. We couldn't imagine painting over something so soon after she had sprayed it. We had visited Katharina in her studio several times; she made suggestions, and we were in very close conversation when Rolf fell ill. Then our energies were redirected towards fighting his cancer.

When I started to go out again, I ran into Katharina one day and was able to tell her why it had been impossible for us to continue the conversation. A few years later, I purchased her small polystyrene sculpture from Barbara Gross [*Untitled*, 2006]. I found the work engaging because one doesn't immediately perceive it as a sculpture, but rather as an unusually shaped object that offers countless surfaces on which paint can land. It's truly extraordinary how the paint forms a translucent film or also puddles on surfaces that tilt and curve in different ways; how it runs or drips in all directions, offers various views that reflect how Katharina turned the work as she sprayed it. At the same time, it is as jagged as a meteorite, without a defined shape.

In 2011, I finally found the courage to commission a wall painting from Katharina. I offered her a choice of two spaces: the music room on the third floor as well as the living room on the fourth floor. I didn't want to pin her to a decision, but I did hope that she would choose the fourth floor, because I imagined her work as an excellent response to Frank Stella, whose relief from his *Moby Dick* series extends in all directions into the room and offers numerous viewpoints, embodying a kind of never-ending search in the cosmos. Thanks to her approach to the architecture, Katharina really set the whole space in motion. She not only developed a wonderful response to Frank Stella, she surpassed his efforts in making the entire room begin to vibrate. *As told to Isabel Parkes*

Can you tell me about making your first wall painting?

Before making what many consider my first wall painting, at Kunsthalle Bern [*Untitled*, 1998], I had produced wall paintings with paintbrushes but felt unsatisfied by how my brush was stopped by a surface's changes, for example, where the floor met the wall. I'd already had some experience with spray paint when I lived in France in the early nineties, because at the time, many people there made spray paintings and cartoons. When I saw the space in Bern, I knew I didn't want to make a painting that behaved within the parameters of a surface, and the idea of spraying came back to me.

Can you tell me about what catalyzed your departure from representational painting?

In the process of painting, there are moments where you go away from the painting to pick up a color. Within those few minutes, before you return to the painting, your mind changes and starts to do something internal with the painting.

I started to become more interested in this process, and I realized that my decision-making was hugely changed by this gap that I could create by leaving a painting alone, going to my paints, and then coming back to the painting. It wasn't just related to what I saw on the canvas or what I saw beyond it, but also to my thoughts when I moved away from the work. I grew interested in the freedom of spatial movement that accompanies not having to represent a certain recognizable feature or form.

What are some other parameters you work within?

I'm interested in having parameters set when I start out rather than working towards them. There are quite a lot of painters who provoke in me the question of where a painting ends. These include [Barnett] Newman and [Jackson] Pollock, but I'm also influenced by European painters like Monet, for example how he handles the moment when the image starts to fade and move beyond the edges of the canvas. One can imagine the painting only shows a glimpse of something that was visually there when it was painted. Monet is also hugely connected to color, far more even than Pollock. Pollock for me is more about the graphic image.

Perhaps also about the exponential quality of imagination.

That's a good observation, because it's essential to the notion of parameter, particularly as something that is not necessarily physical.

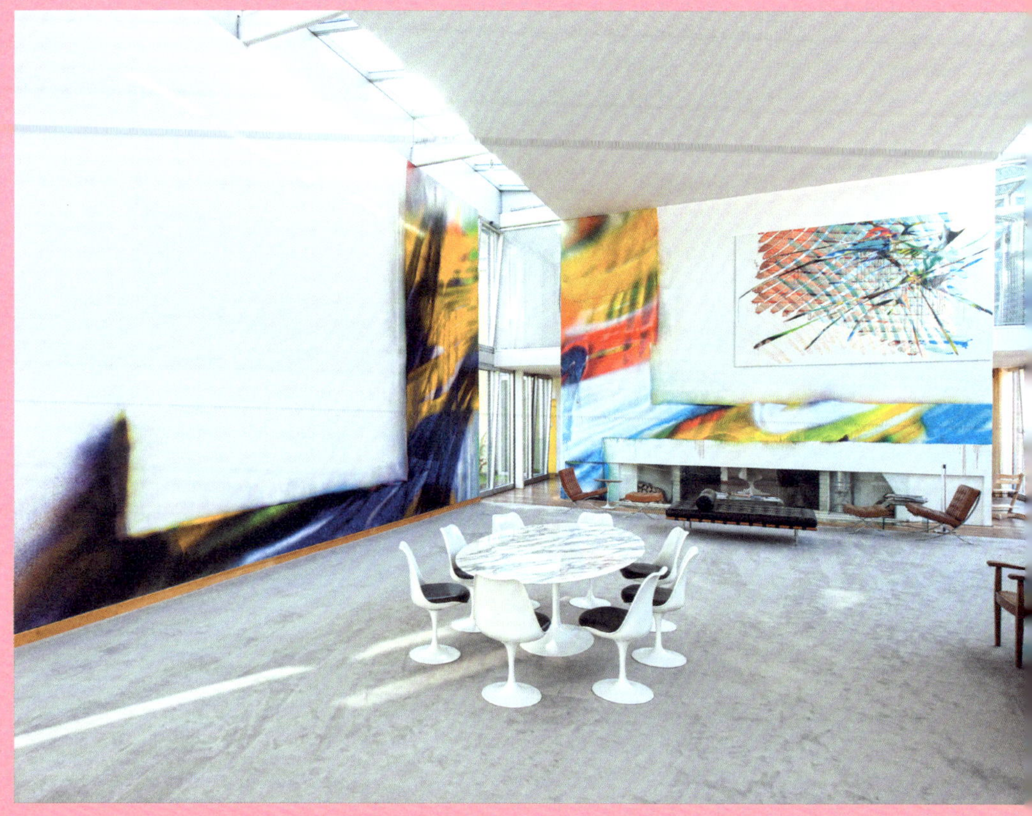

Sie trocken ihre Knie mit einem Kissen
(They dry their knees with a pillow), 2012
Untitled, 2011
Sammlung Hoffmann Installation XVI, 2012–13

And not necessarily a limit. I find that you don't work against limits as much as in or on them.

I've started to understand how a border can be a point at which two very different energies converge, get denser, and shrink. As a space it is hyper-packed and urgent. I like to go in there, almost like going into a crease between pillows. It's where negotiation takes place, where you have to deal with energies that seem to exclude one another.

This conversation seems parallel to one about abstraction and the way it both negates and preserves reality. A Monet haystack is to me both preserving an image of what he saw in a field and transforming it. I see that in your work.

I understand abstraction more as without reference to any image. As a leap towards nowhere or from somewhere—perhaps into that border or something that you don't know.

And still, instinctively, viewers seek something to identify, which your work largely defies.

Yes, and in this sense, my site-related and my studio work occupy different categories. My site-related work is embedded in existing imagery, for example a surface of trees, soil, grass, or rubble. For example, my MoMA PS1 piece [*Rockaway*, 2016] was not simply a house, but one stripped bare and with sand half coming in, half out. If one looks for a reference, what comes to mind first: Hurricane Sandy or Abstract Expressionism? You might see its orange and red colors as a sunset. Then you have to look at it to realize it's not a sunset. If you look for the illusion, in the sense of "something looks like," then you might take it for a red herring.

Similes and metaphors can also be dangerous in language.

Exactly, and we have to discover that they do not work. But I find the idea of imagination and illusion, the sense of "what if," fascinating.

A moment of potential.

Yes.

And ideally potential is limitless.

Yes. Ideally, we have x numbers of alternatives, although we tend to only see the one that we can identify, or in other words, that one that we know. That's why I try to propose multiple possibilities. I try to embed image into image into image.

I think my work created in the studio is different, not only in size, but also in method and in its relationship to the surface.

Tell me more about that process. How does something on canvas such as *Untitled* (2011) start as opposed to the wall painting in the Sammlung Hoffmann, *They dry their knees with a pillow* (2012)?

I worked with stencils for that particular painting on canvas. I wanted to minimize the overall painted space between distinct layers and to have mutually exclusive surfaces that could cut into something I couldn't classify spatially. My understanding of the surface started to change with this work. The surface is not just the flatness of the canvas onto which I can paint many layers, but also where I can actually hide layers. I think it has to do with how I'm now understanding the border as a packed space. My canvas works enable me to explore how packed and charged a surface can be.

Do you think that possibility is unique to working on a canvas? I believe the first work Erika acquired of yours was a sculpture (*Untitled*, 2006).

Yes, canvas has a different ability to both maximize and minimize a smaller space. If you were to unpack a two- by three-meter canvas covered in layers, you would end up with a surface of about one hundred square meters. The cluster you can generate in terms of time and space on a canvas totally defies the idea of chronological or binary thinking. What you then see or perceive is another matter. I think that is one of the quintessential qualities of painting: that is has a different approach towards time. The surface of a canvas can expose this more than a sculpted surface. The sculpted surface has different issues, for example the authenticity of material.

Your former professor Gotthard Graubner was also thinking about these issues.

Yes, but they came to my mind later. I had many different teachers and studied a long time. Early on in my first year, I had a teacher who was a sculptor who used paint. I next had a really great teacher, a conceptual sculptor called Reiner Ruthenbeck, who was interested in a work's spiritual quality and in how the invisible strengthens the visible. Graubner pointed towards the power of color, independent from what it depicted. He was not a theoretical thinker. His father made violins, so he was a very musical kid and apparently could whistle whole symphonies. In German we would say *musisch*—not just musical but he could absorb life in an unusual way.

How did architecture become interesting to you?

Painting has not been independent of architecture for very long in terms of history. It's a radical thought but a relatively new one that the painting is not part of a space. I lived in Florence for a year and got totally into the relationship between urban, architectural, and painted space. It's such an everyday experience to see painting there, whether it is an orange house, a sign, or frescos in a church. I find the idea that painting is an isolated system misleading and uninteresting.

How does your approach to painting change as the spaces in which you work get larger?

It has to do with whether I end up in a battle against hugeness or if I can come up with a proposal that hopefully, cleverly changes our and its own relationship to painted space. Overall, my process is not technical as much as mental, and about reassessing decisions. That's what I like so much about painting: that you are able to start with a very decided set of elements, but then when you are only two steps out the door you are suddenly in a situation that was impossible to anticipate.

Sounds precarious.

Yes, and you imagine that something could happen to you that you might love to experience, but also know that it is or could be dangerous. Painting demands a kind of alertness to both risk and safety. *(pauses)*

I had a really great experience the other day when I was preparing for a show. I wanted a certain number of paintings that had a certain density, and it was not working. Everything was feeling stuck. As I went to the studio one morning, traffic was sticky and that put me in an even worse mood. Then I started thinking, wow what if now an accident occurred and my windshield broke, then I would possibly get glass in my eye and not even be able to paint! Nothing happened.

The next day, I came out of my house, in a rush, but I had locked my only car keys inside my car, which is old and not electronic. I called a mechanic, who suggested smashing the window. He gave me instructions on how to do it, so I smashed the window and it felt so good! The whole car was full of glass. Somehow, what I had imagined had occurred, but in a totally different way than I had first thought. That was fascinating. Things then felt unblocked, and I started to paint better. For me, this idea that wishing for something can be both dangerous and not, was captured then and there.

In a moment like that you are facing fear.

Yes, but also in play mode. It was as if I was acting it out.

Have you had that kind of experience in front of painting that is not your own?

No, but I have it sometimes when I read books and experience how courageously some authors use language.

I think of Cervantes when you say that. Who do you have in mind?

Yes, *Don Quixote* is a good example, or the introduction of *Lolita*. I think painting is so familiar to me that I often don't have that feeling of danger. Sometimes it occurs if something totally changes. But the idea of process is that you are in constant negotiation with the newly acquired information that comes your way. Resistance comes from the material. You have a certain imagination of what you could do or what you could try, and then you do it, and it is totally different from what you imagined.

Which is perhaps part of what you were describing earlier when you said that you try to take a few minutes in between painting.

Yeah, but I don't have that anymore. I find that painting and thinking are so closely related–you don't execute a thought, you are thinking and painting at the same time.

It's kind of sad for viewers to miss out on this.

Yes, but they could have the same experience in looking at the work.

Are you optimistic?

I like to think that I'm an optimist, but I hear myself complaining a lot. I have no reason to.

Self-awareness can be cruel. And to be able to reassess decisions is a great privilege but also limiting.

I think there's a difference if you judge or if you don't. That's something great that I discovered for myself through painting: I am constantly making decisions and if I take time to judge them while I work, then I really make it more difficult. I lose the connection to my decision-flow.

To be non-judgmental of oneself is difficult!

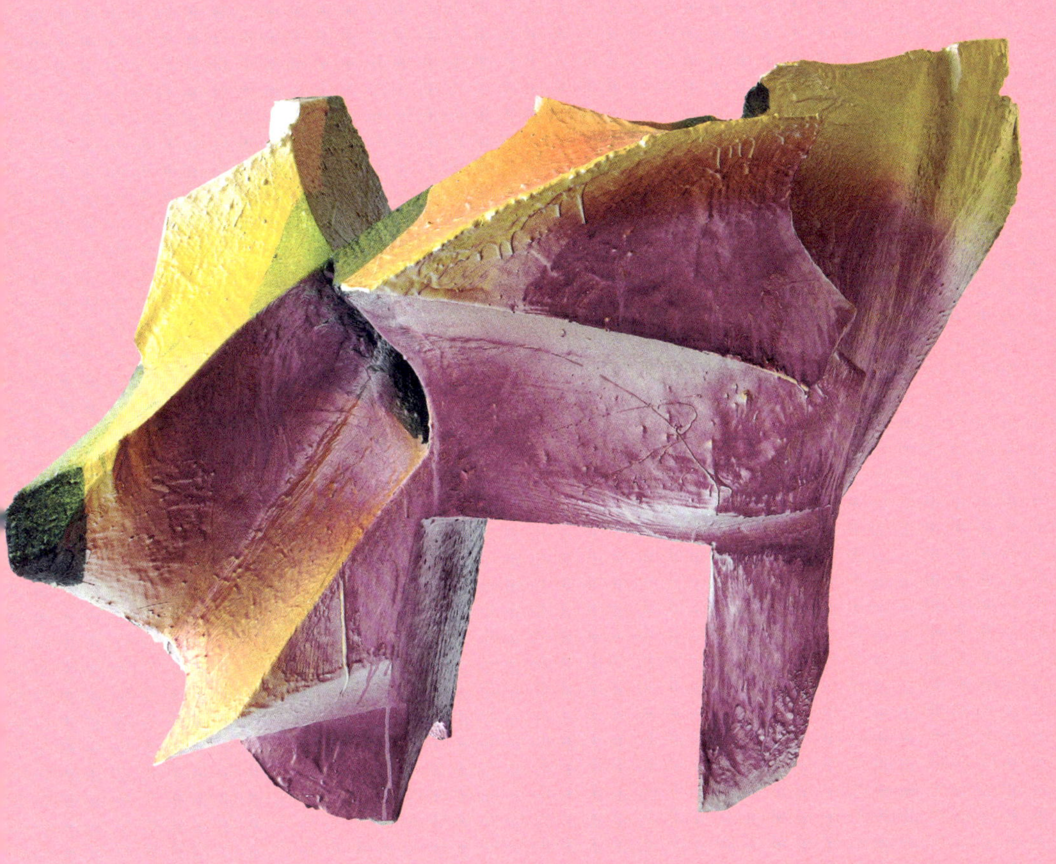

Untitled, 2006

It relates to where you and your activity are placed within the field in which you work. I feel this establishes another fundamental difference between me and someone like Pollock. I think he understood himself as the author, on top of the hierarchy, and the field in which he worked. Maybe he said he worked from within, but I guess he would still have said that he made the work. I would say that I am not a different element from the paints, the surface, the circumstances, the machine, the weather. They are as much agents as I am. I am within them. I try to see the relationship between these elements, which makes judging a different issue. It changes how you discuss the work with yourself.

I'm still imagining the moment in which you smashed your car window and the one in which you imagined your windshield being smashed, and wondering if that's what made it so cathartic. You already knew. You'd had that discussion with yourself.

Yes, I was prepared! In a sense, as a painter you can reverse time, and that is something I am very used to. It's not only that you can judge or find a perspective in which you say, "No I don't like it. I will work over it," but also that you have this experience of the reversibility of all things. When you are immersed in a certain group of different elements, you know that one can become dominant and as the work evolves, a different one grows dominant, and so on. It's not an issue of hierarchy or even dominance, but of fluidity. All the elements are changing all the time and that's what makes judgement such a relative activity.

RONI HORN

We first saw Roni Horn's work in Cologne at Rafael Jablonka's gallery in the mid-nineties. After the opening, we ate dinner with Rafael and Roni, and talked. Roni was open and communicative. She liked to talk, although I didn't understand everything she said because her way of speaking wasn't like the American English I had encountered thus far—either that or I had never operated at an intellectual level like hers before. We actually didn't notice that she looked like a young man—that was a characteristic I read about in newspaper articles attempting to categorize her, I suppose. We thought she was an incredible person. After some consideration, we acquired her aluminum sculpture *Blake's Burn* (1994–95) from that exhibition. The two cuboid figures, one lying on top of the other and made of raw grey aluminum, reminded us of Judd's Minimalism. Not only this, but the work's gleaming yellow plastic letters, embedded in either side of the sculpture imbued it with an eerie ambiance. Reading over William Blake's 1794 poem, *The Tyger*, the repeated "fearful symmetry" etched itself in our memories as something threatening.

After Rafael moved his gallery to Lindenstrasse, he showed Roni's *Deeps and Skies* (1995–96) on the ground floor. We immediately fell in love with this blue glass block whose sides seem covered in ice and whose top surface is reflective and clear, making you want to dip your hands in it like water. Without knowing exactly what we were getting ourselves into, we were captivated by its aesthetic. It was similar with *Paired Gold Mats – For Ross and Felix* (1995), which Roni showed us when we visited her studio in New York. We were instantly taken just by looking at the two sheets of gold foil, as warm light glowed along their wrinkled edges. This was before we even understood the title. Of course, we knew the story of Felix Gonzalez-Torres and his boyfriend Ross—a billboard by Felix that conveys his grief about Ross covered the wall of our dining room in Cologne at the time. We understood Roni's *Gold Mats* as a response, by a friend, to Felix's installation that consists of candies wrapped in gold-colored cellophane. Like all of his works, this is "*Untitled*," but it has a subtitle in parentheses: *Placebo-Landscape-For Roni* (1993).

I have a difficult time describing Roni's work. I am intrigued by how she plays with what she calls "shifting meaning," with identities, with possibilities of transformation, with change as a state itself, and not least of all by the emotional weight of minimalist shapes. When faced with uncertainty, we ask ourselves what it is we are actually seeing.

A friend of mine, an art historian, told me once that she finds Roni's work too cryptic. She felt Roni was too strongly oriented towards other artists, could only be understood with respect to them, and hardly at all by a more general public. I couldn't agree less with this opinion! My friend seemed suspicious of the fact that Roni might make herself mysterious.

I think it is precisely this mystery that captivates me in her work. I was only able to understand why Emily Dickinson's poems are so important to Roni when I read them myself: no rhyme, no closure, open to manifold interpretations. Roni's work continues to totally intrigue because it offers or suggests something that you cannot put your finger on, it always keeps going, simply impossible to grasp. *As told to Isabel Parkes*

How did you first meet Erika and Rolf Hoffmann?

I'm not sure I'm going to be able to remember, but I think it was connected to gallerist Rafael Jablonka. How do you prepare for this? *(pauses)* I don't really remember our first meeting in my studio, but I do remember talking with Erika a lot. She would come before or after my openings, when it was quiet, and we would just look at the work together and talk about it.

What were those early conversations like?

I think that we recognized each other, that's all. I had the sense that Erika understood me in such a way that I didn't need to talk about myself. Not that it was personal—although it bleeds into that—but we were speaking a language that we could each relate to. It wasn't necessarily verbal. I would say my connection was very strong with her.

At some point, she was coming more to the States and I spent time with her when I did a show at Dia Beacon [*Roni Horn: Part I and Part II*, 2001–02], which happened after Rolf had passed. She was fragile at that moment, but lovely as ever. I could feel her difficulty in carrying on. Not that she wouldn't carry on exactly as she wished, but that she was gathering forces to go forward. At some point she asked me to contribute something to the memorial for Rolf and I sent a recording.

Why did you choose *Saying Water* (2001)?

Water is a subject that has relevance to everything. So, if someone says the primary subject of the piece is water, or a kind of litany of consciousness around water, I would say that the work is about continuity. It's about connection. It's about endlessly renewed identity. I felt those subjects would be meaningful without talking specifically about Rolf, because I also feel that at memorials, speaking specifically about the person is not always something I'm able to do. Sometimes I don't want to do it because that level—that looking back—doesn't really mean anything.

I remember this from my mother's memorial as well, where that way of speaking just didn't work for me. I don't think I really knew Rolf that well and I didn't want to try to create something that had specificity that wasn't real. For me that would be disrespectful, so I decided to do something more general, which for me can be just as meaningful.

I use the word litany with *Saying Water* because there is a sad, difficult element to it, which is the way water covers darkness or the way water exposes the darkness of life. I certainly don't imagine death as a darkness, but I do understand an ongoing sense of change that is accurately measured in water's flow.

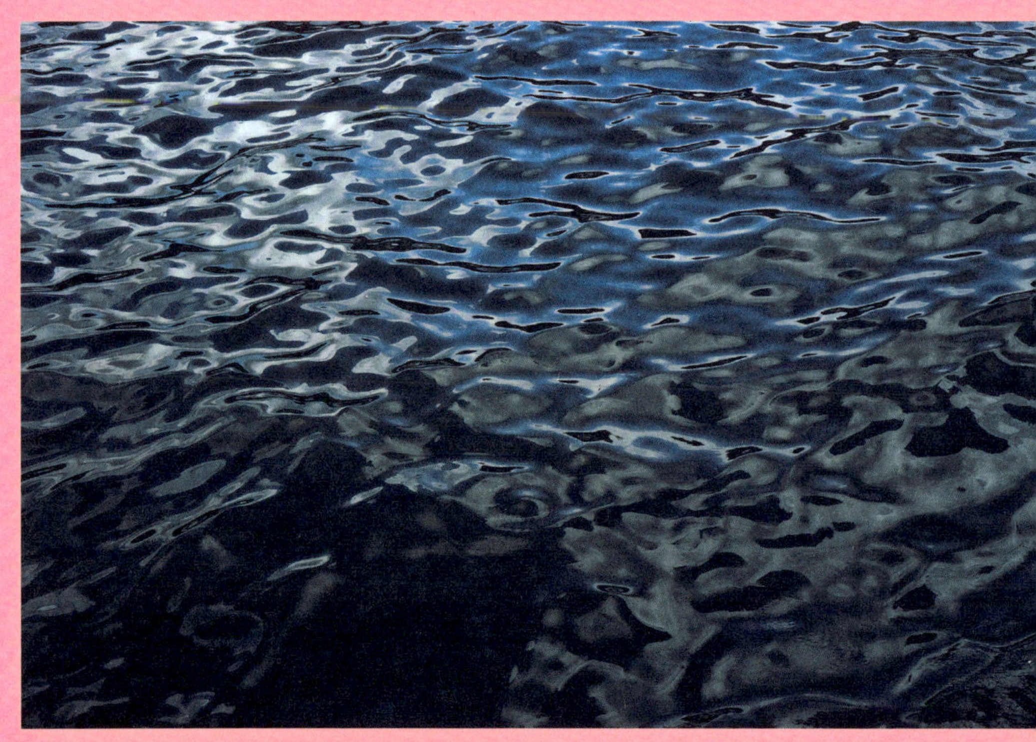

From Some Thames, 2000 (detail)

Using the general to talk about something specific is an interesting frame for your work. It feels like you did the opposite with your memorial to Felix Gonzalez-Torres.

I knew Felix very well and not only that, he asked me to speak at his memorial. That made it essential for me to find something to say that was true, simply true, to me and to him. I tried to observe him and write down what I observed of his extraordinary persona and work, that's all. I didn't get into anything personal. It was all pretty much through the work.

Which in his case seems mostly inseparable from the person.

Absolutely.

Rereading the text you wrote, I often pause at the line about, "observ[ing] the world becoming more present to itself." This feels like a guiding line in your work. Are you aware of your legacy as an artist?

I'm not putting a lot of effort into it if that's what you mean! I'm not sure what the question is.

I'm thinking of legacy in terms of the cumulative way you work. Like Felix's practice, yours seems to grow more into itself, more present, over time.

What I can say is that my work is bound to the actual, but I think to a great extent the actual is over. That sounds histrionic, but I don't think it is. There's a tipping point with the destruction of nature, whereby a new generation is really not growing up with nature, so it has no need for it. The new generation might even fear it. A great distance—and a way forward without nature—is created. Nature is the ultimate actual in terms of scale.

For me this relates closely to the thinning out of individual awareness, attention, and capacity. By this I mean that you're fragmenting consciousness to such an extent that the idea of intelligence shifts. Consciousness is being profoundly weakened in a way that enables artificial intelligence to become an appealing factor as opposed to a challenge.

Your work toes the related lines of materiality and immateriality, description and indescribability, which I consider paradoxes around consciousness. Each requires time to emerge, but my generation generally wants to consume and continue. How do you focus on the actual as the demand for your work and the scale of your productions have each increased over the decades?

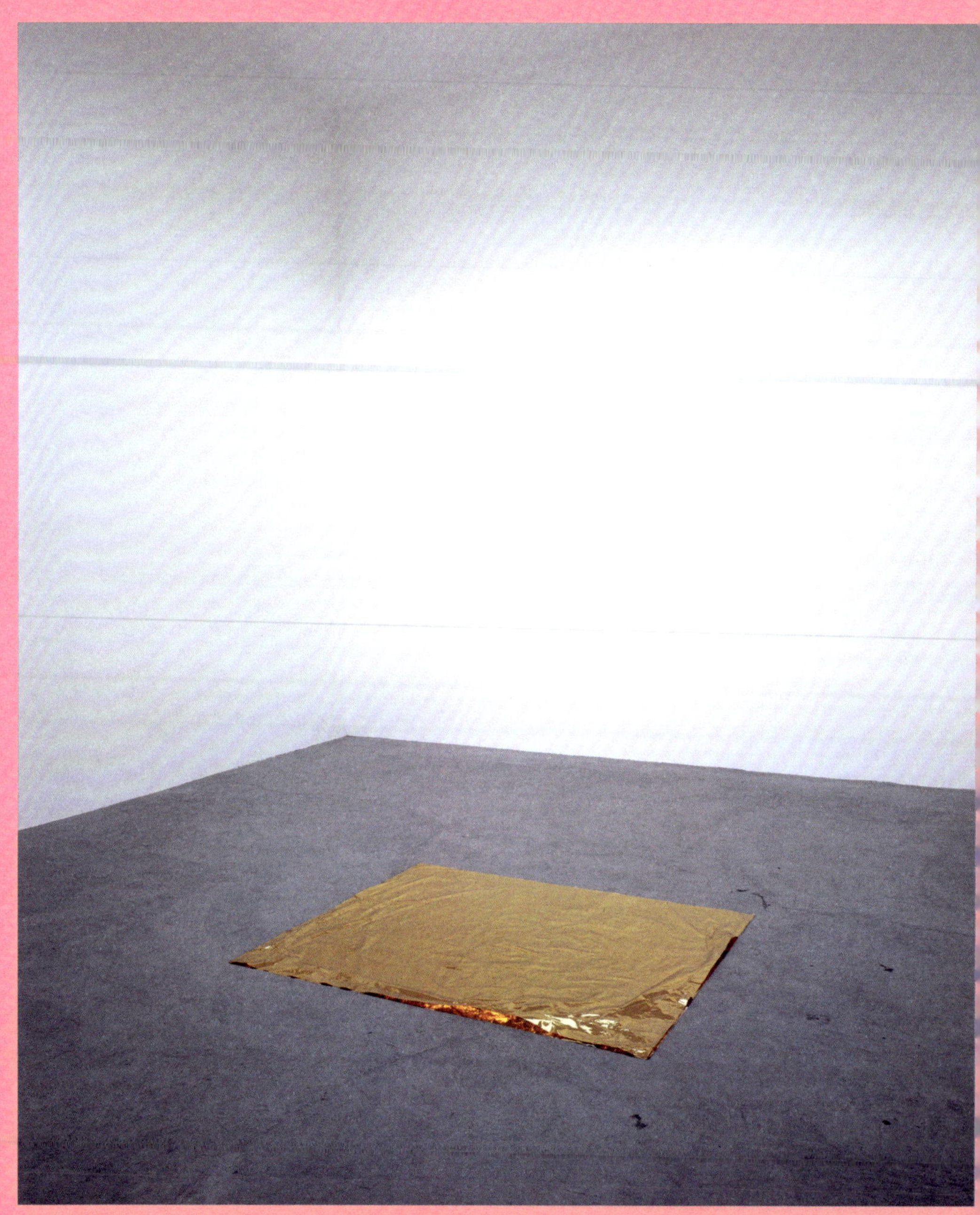

Paired Gold Mats – For Ross and Felix, 1995

I've always thought that the meaning of the work is directly informed by the experience of it. That is where it starts and hopefully it doesn't stop, because experience usually doesn't. I keep things very empirical, as the empirical is something everybody shares. For me that remains meaningful.

As far as being in big galleries and producing goes, I would just say that the market is bigger than you are, and so either you're informing it or you're—well, nobody's independent of it. My education in the art world started with an idea of galleries that was very different than what they are now. My very early experiences were with people who were highly knowledgeable and deeply passionate about the work itself and the financial side of it was very, very attenuated. There was no hope! You would never go into the arts if you wanted to be rich, which I think has changed now. At the time I was first showing, it was about education. It was about really offering a life and a meaningful experience.

I saw art as something that was essential to the well-being of oneself and also of society. Once money started coming in, art was hijacked by a different language and economic dynamic that made invention unnecessary and even undesirable, because invention isn't something that a lot of people recognize. It sometimes takes years for things to be present in their full content. But the idea of production, of things that you could just sell, that's much easier to get your head around and unfortunately, it's not just dealers that are involved. At some point going to a gallery lost any experiential value. Today, the use of art fairs and the internet to sell or present art is hostile to anything involving the actual. I've stayed with the experiential as the key to my work, but I'm not ignorant of the forces that are informing an individual's experience today, and they're coming from a more virtual space.

What have you observed?

For one, unfortunately, so much of the new generation comes in with no reference for geography—north, south, east, west *(pauses)*, really basic things. I know that when I get into a car and I use its navigation system, I always have a reference for the directions separate from the navigation system. These systems are not really giving directions in the sense that they're assuming there's nothing out there except what they're telling you is out there, and I don't have that faith.

If you consider [Andy] Warhol or [Joseph] Beuys, you see two men who both founded their work in their own image. You can see that Warhol was the winner, if you want to put it that way, because his image was connected to distribution in the sense of an economy. Beuys was connected to education, which doesn't go far anymore. I'm not being cynical, but I am observing the forces that Warhol made central to his work.

Whether he did so knowingly is irrelevant, because it's done, and it was very effective. I think that Beuys was not interested in capitalism the way Warhol was. I think Warhol was in the sense that he called his studio a factory, which already tells you something. That idea of legacy is not somewhere I'm able to go.

I don't like to put my physical presence out there much. I'm a very, very solitary and private person. Well, a very solitary person because privacy is over. Solitude is over too because you can't really only have one without the other. There are so many other things that are important to me that are really hanging by a thread, like the idea of getting lost.

How do you find solitude today?

I'm not sure that I do! I think it's relative. I know that as long as I use technology, people know more about me than I think they do, in a way that's uncomfortable for me. Whether it's simply location—well it's never simply anything anymore, because frequency and temporal elements enter the equation and take away anonymity.

Virtual time relates to virtual space in a completely different way than either exists physically.

Yeah. You know, when I was in Iceland a lot, I was always flirting with getting lost because I didn't have technology. I didn't pick a cell phone for quite a few years after they became available, but once getting lost became voluntary, it became an oxymoron. You don't choose to get lost. You get lost because you've taken a risk. And that was what drew me to being in Iceland and alone all those years. And when I was doing that, I felt a solitude that I no longer feel anywhere in my life.

How do you find focus, your individual attention, today?

I have to work to hold onto it. I don't answer the phone unless I choose to use it or make a phone appointment. I don't interact with the phone spontaneously at all. And that takes away that level of distraction that some people are more comfortable with. I have a lot of friends who still interrupt conversations or dinners to deal with their phones and I would never do that. Nothing in my life has that kind of pressing need time-wise, even though I constantly see things speeding up. I think there are so many options for every given thing, that in a way, options are a very corrosive force. Options aren't really adding anything, they're just breaking things down.

When everything becomes an option, nothing actually is one.

Let's be concrete: if you look at what's happened with travel options, you see that they've destroyed actually connecting to people. Now you can go from Kalamazoo, Michigan to Paris with a direct flight, and anywhere else, at any time. What that does is like the Internet: people expect you to be on, and it makes it very complicated to not travel. I've been traveling a hell of a lot and I'm somebody who's trying not to. The only thing I have now is to put somebody between me and the travel and have them do it. I don't know what the solution is, but attention is no longer there. Attention is now something you have to achieve.

I feel this idea about attention and options relates to how information is transmitted and received constantly today. I find your work both offers a lot of information and none, which is a contradiction some people find unsettling. I'm thinking of a piece like *Deeps and Skies* (1995–96), which, in my experience of giving tours in the Sammlung Hoffmann, would often incite visitors to ask about its weight or material or value.

Yeah, there is a kind of reticence in that work, but it is reticent in light of all that it plays to the viewer, if they pay attention, so I don't know how reticent that is. You do need to be there as a human being, meaning with all your senses and your consciousness, and people aren't really anymore. This is what I mean about artificial intelligence becoming an appealing option as people choose to abandon their consciousness!

You get people bingeing things, streaming stuff, constantly on iPads or iPhones, playing games, whatever it is to get you through. It's the thing of killing time. When most of life for some people is killing time, the values shift from being where you are, when you're there, to not being there at all. Now enter artificial intelligence, because we don't need you to be there. Nothing needs anyone to be there with their sentience. They can just not be there at all. That's what artificial intelligence is to some extent.

I see humanity being broken down this way, almost by choice. I don't want to make a judgment call, but you do. I do feel the values have shifted so that, for example, the way privacy has been given away, renders surveillance absolutely legal. People's thoughtlessness on these fronts is part of the reality of our time.

When did you last see something that reminded you of the actual or experiential qualities you mentioned earlier as central to your work?

Well in the arts it's not so frequent with younger generation material. First of all, for a lot of the younger generation's work, I need time with it. I'm not somebody who has an opinion about an artist based on one or two shows or one or two performances. For me, culture takes time. It takes time for an individual's voice to be present, and I think that one of the things that happens with a highly monetized culture, is that people don't have time. So, if you're not there at the starting gate, then you're not there at all. If your show isn't making money, it's out.

When I was a kid, I used to read these books about India, and philosophy and theology were always in the same phrase, inseparable. These books would explain cycles of increasing deterioration, which I never understood back then.

A kind of spiritual entropy.

Yeah, like things fall apart. And they make me think, I grew up me, Roni Horn, New York, Jewish middle class, in America. I had all the options. I thought, "Look at capitalism! They actually reward you for inventing something! This is fantastic!" And then it just turned into this monstrosity of exploitation. That's the experience that I live.

Some would say you're in the eye of that storm in New York, and while you've been asked many times about what Iceland's landscape has done for your work, I wonder what New York has done.

It's been a long time since New York was the eye of the storm for me. I spent most of my life in New York and it had an edge that it doesn't have now. That edge interested me even though it was threatening and difficult to deal with. It was engaging and it was a life force.

I recently read a well-known biography by Robert Caro about Robert Moses, who is referred to as "The Master Builder" of New York. For me the book provided so much context for understanding how a relationship to corruption is endemic to this city, certainly in a male-dominated world. One thing that Robert Moses did that was so deeply destructive to New York was to refuse the development of mass transit in any way. A lot of what we live now is his failure as an urban planner.

How has the city itself or rather its failed urban plan impacted your work?

I think the street is in my work but it's not announcing itself. It's behind the scenes of things that went into putting the work together and what it required. It's a whole other conversation!

What are you working on currently?

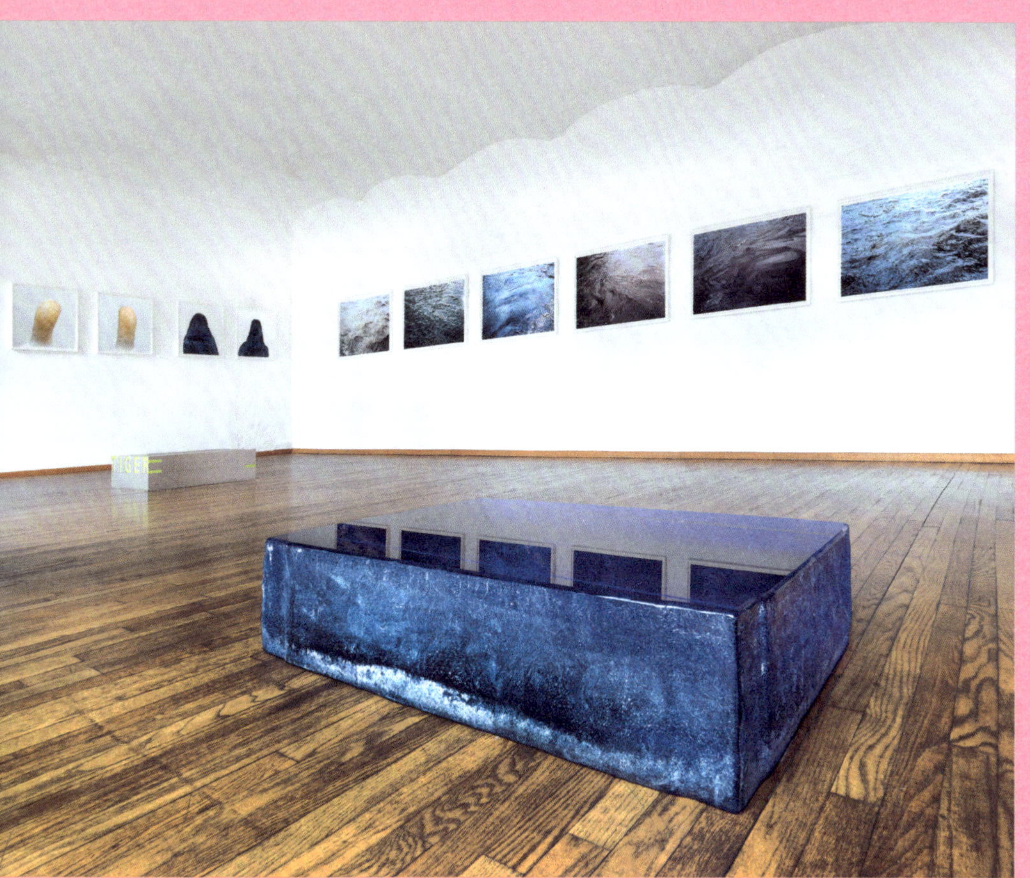

Deeps and Skies, 1995–96
Blake's Burn, 1994–95
Untitled #3, 1998
Untitled #1 (Ravens), 1998
From Some Thames, 2000
Sammlung Hoffmann Installation XVI, 2012–13

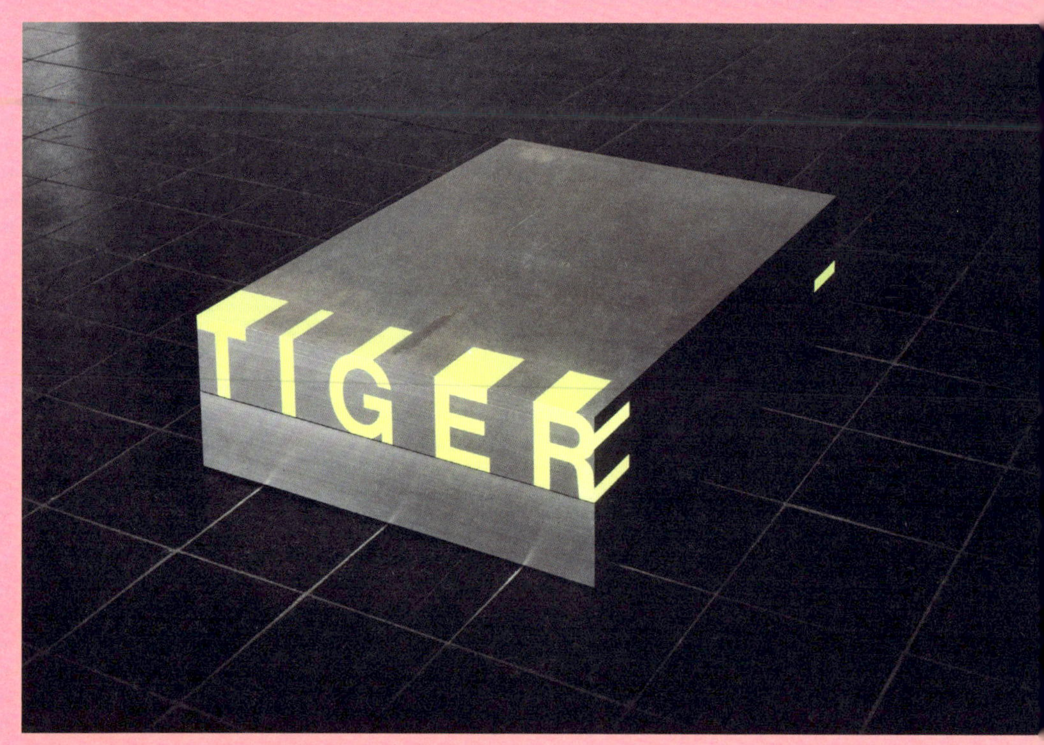

Blake's Burn, 1994–95

I'm working on a few things but the one that I'm focused on now is a project in northern Norway which is part of the country's so-called tourist routes. Some other artists and I have been invited to do things to encourage people to go up into these remote areas. It's been a very long story, but we've finally arrived at the point where the construction is happening, and that involves the installation of a *Water Double*, which is a pair of very, very large glass units that are five tons each. They're going to sit in a small purpose-built building with no infrastructure so that you can go 24/7. Whether by moonlight or by sunlight, it remains a simple, vernacular style building of turf and wood construction.

I've become less interested in doing gallery shows. You just have to keep the balance between the basic survival of it all. I don't think about the legacy, but I know what it takes to get something to exist.

KATARZYNA KOZYRA

Katarzyna Kozyra's work always amazes me, both in terms of the topics it deals with and because of the vehemence within it, not to mention the determination with which Katarzyna pursues her subjects. It seems that for Katarzyna, boundaries of time or energy simply don't exist. Like many others, she suffers as she faces contemporary Polish society.

Although I visited Poland for the first time in 1996, I had been interested in what was going on with our Eastern neighbors for many years, and had been corresponding sporadically with Polish art historian Szymon Bojko since 1980. Szymon not only wrote to me about the *Solidarność*—of course I had to ignore the blacked-out, censored parts of our letters—but also referred me to artists such as Tamara de Lempicka, Teresa Murak, and Teresa Tyszkiewicz, as I was interested in clothing, beyond the world of fashion. Of course, Katarzyna Kozyra and Zuzanna Janin, who I met in Warsaw in 1996, don't belong to this generation of artists, but the one that followed.

Katarzyna and I got to know each other in an unconventional way in the spring of 2005. I heard a voice I didn't recognize on the phone, and although I couldn't make out the name, I understood that she was an artist and had just installed a work in the exhibition *Über Schönheit* (On Beauty) at the Haus der Kulturen der Welt [in Berlin], which she wanted to show me. I found it quite original that someone would just call me—that someone had looked up my private phone number—and I felt adventurous enough to make an appointment with this person.

We met at the HKW at 10 am, but it turned out that on Sundays they opened at 11. So, we went to the café and Katarzyna told me how she came to create the work and what kinds of things she did in general. Thus, I was able to learn a few things before we watched her video, *The Rite of Spring* (1999–2002) together. I was disappointed by the way it was presented sculpturally and found the black wooden boxes clunky in relation to the small screens inside them. But I recalled with interest how Katarzyna transformed the myth of *The Rite of Spring*—and had a good memory of her as a person.

Months later, when she hosted a spaghetti dinner for friends and invited me, I learned that there was a smaller version of *The Rite of Spring*, which was actually the first version. I was really happy to receive it at home and find that an employee from Warsaw's Zachęta museum would install it. I found it fascinating how in the work, Katarzyna takes up not only the gender discussion from the original myth, *Le sacre du printemps*, but also the topic of age. In her reinterpretation of the ritual, it's not a beautiful young girl who is sacrificed, but ugly old people; she also swapped the typical sex attributes of men and women.

Another aspect that interested me was the production of stop-motion photographs as part of the six-channel video installation. I could hardly imagine how Katarzyna spent months on her hands and knees, crawling around on the floor next to elderly people as they lay there—her "dancers"—in order to arrange their bodies and limbs as dictated by Nijinsky's choreography. Her next step was always to stand up, take each shot, and re-stage thousands of movement-moments. She did all of this alone, except for the synchronization with Stravinsky's music, and all with incredible tenacity. How daring it is to undertake this kind of animation—even if the result is only thirty-two seconds long—and what obsessiveness is required to see it through! *As told to Isabel Parkes*

I just called Erika at home. I suppose it surprised her that an artist would pick up the phone and call, but nevertheless, she agreed to meet. That was around 2004.

What did you say on the phone?

That I was an artist and had heard that she wanted to meet me. That's what I had been told at HAU (Hebbel am Ufer Theater, Berlin), although later it turned out that wasn't really true. I wanted to meet her in any case.

At that time, my video installation *The Rite of Spring* (1999–2002) was being exhibited at Haus der Kulturen der Welt, so Erika and I arranged to meet there at 10 am. When I arrived, I realized that it didn't open until 11. Erika had come by bike, but I didn't notice that she was already there. We found each other eventually and went upstairs to the café. I told her about the work, which was an unusual piece for me at the time. I think I was still under its spell, soaked in it like a sponge. We watched it together and then, after that first meeting, some time passed before I called her again. Erika told me that she was stuck at home with a broken leg, so I went to see her and that's really how our friendship began. We started cooking together at her home, which is something that we've continued to do over the years.

What do you cook together?

I've learned a lot of recipes from Erika, including very simple ones. I like how she adapts recipes inherited from her mother, which we today call eating locally or seasonally. One of the recipes I most enjoy making is braised pumpkin with leeks and buckwheat. One simply learns from Erika. She possesses a mixture of immense curiosity, humility, and adventurousness, plus she has a lot of human experience. You can always count on her. That she's donating her collection to Dresden is a sign that she is a truly thoughtful and aware person. She understands that art lives for art. She also dearly values artists—and artists as people.

When did you realize you were an artist?

I was very young. I'm not sure I knew it, but I could feel it. It's probably why I was punished so frequently. No one around me seemed to recognize it.

What do you mean by punished?

Psychologically and physically. I grew up mostly in Austria and Germany, but my parents were Polish. My first installation was a winter landscape in our apartment in Vienna, made when

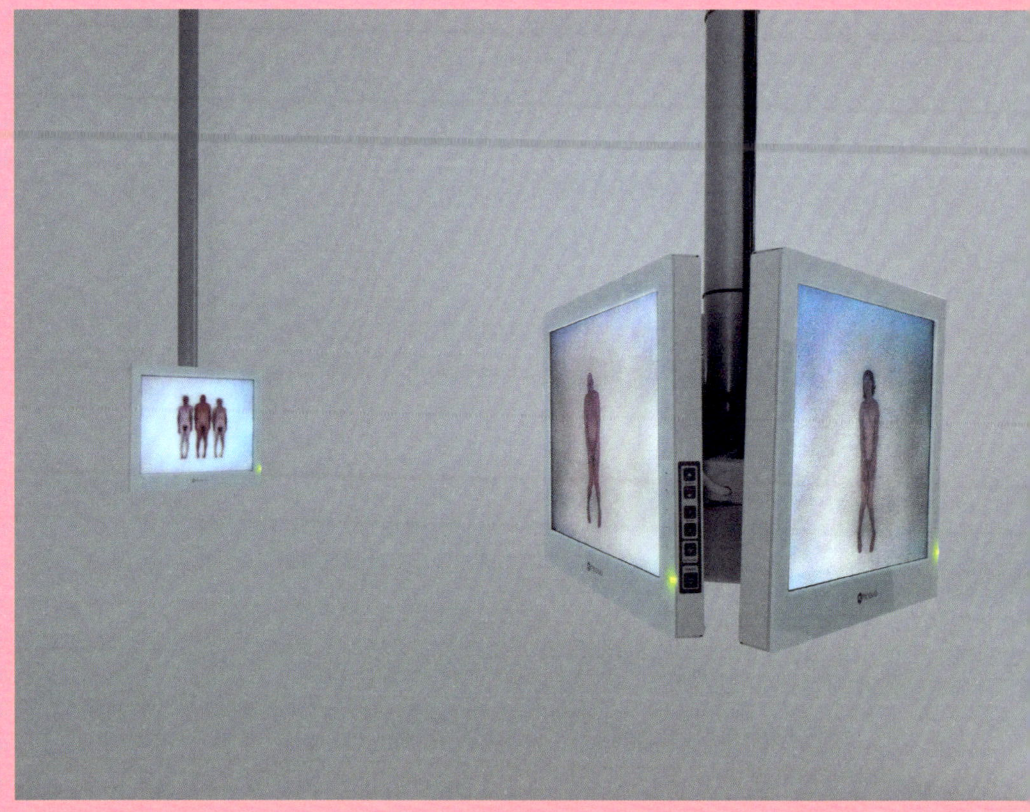

The Rite of Spring, 1999
Sammlung Hoffmann Installation XVIII, 2014–15

I was four or five years old. My mother was lying on the sofa pretending to sleep, but I noticed that she was blinking. I tore up all the paper I could find and rolled it into little balls that I scattered across the living room. Everything turned white. My mom pretended to wake up and I exclaimed, "Look, Mommy, it snowed!" She started scolding me and even beat me. That was my first performance.

What was school like for you?

I was unable to write for a very long time. I was dyslexic, but at the time my disability was considered idiocy. My mother thought that she could teach me to write with her fists, and in a manner of speaking, she managed to do so, even if it took a while.

What was Warsaw like when you arrived there?

I was eighteen and it was meant to be a new beginning for me. After trying normal school, I enrolled in a special one, which I had really fought for. In the so-called normal school, I often found myself in conflict with teachers who relied on something like a military system. This included standing up and saluting when addressed by a teacher. *(pauses)* Maybe not saluting exactly, but something very reminiscent of a military drill, probably as had been used in Austria before the war. I remember fighting with a teacher because she wouldn't stop speaking Russian to me even though she knew I didn't understand it. I started answering in German, which was unforgivable at the time. In the new school, I was among musicians, athletes, nuns, and policemen: people who couldn't manage elsewhere for a variety of reasons.

Tell me about your *Pyramid of Animals* (1993). You were punished for that, too.

The art academy was the first moment I felt I was in the right place. *Pyramid of Animals* was my first mature, or let's say intellectual or artistic statement. I went to the veterinary academy as an art student and as a first step, had to convince its director of my idea. I told him that I was planning to do my diploma in art and that I wanted to euthanize a horse, a dog, a cat, and a rooster in order to place one on top of the other and explore the relationship between reality and fairytale. The fairytale comes from *The Bremen Town Musicians* by the Grimm Brothers, from 1819. The flesh or meat of the animals was my secondary concern, while my real subject was sculpture. The work ended up existing between formats—sculpture and video—and the whole process of making it was a surprise.

I didn't know where to place myself, ethically, morally, or aesthetically.

Would you say that you often start with an idea and follow an unfamiliar process?

I often arrive in worlds that I don't know much about. I start by tracking down rules and formats as I seek to understand them. I barge in with my own understanding or misunderstanding. Often, I notice how structured everything is around us as humans. Everything is regulated down to the last detail, but there are also many situations and procedures in which set rules don't fit and it's there, in those situations, that I wend my way. My animal pyramid was a truly enlightening process.

A few years later, in 1996, you brought *Olympia* into the world. Can you describe the process of creating that work?

I was still under the shock of the pyramid process and depressed when I developed *Olympia*. My personal life—my battle with Hodgkin lymphoma—was in all the tabloids. Suddenly the Polish media, which had been so against me during the time of the pyramid work, declared it forgivable that such a young girl might talk about death. Public opinion was totally manipulated so that people could or even should forgive me. I felt almost forced to participate in the 1996 *Olympia* exhibition at Ujazdowski Castle in Warsaw. At the time, I was living alone in an apartment, without insurance, and could not really comprehend reality around me. I call it shock, but I'm still not sure what exactly it was.

Once I had agreed to participate in that exhibition, I began talking to older people, especially older women, and eventually asked a number of them to sit for me. I wanted to see old, or shall we say, deformed bodies. During this time, through the course of my own illness and my doctor, I met a very young girl who had leukemia. Her skin was completely pale, practically alabaster. It was, for lack of a better expression, inspiring to me, and I was taken with her story. I wanted her to play Olympia and to make visible her IV as she underwent treatment. This felt tied to how, in my animal pyramid, a horse had been put to sleep with an IV and we, two women, were now being kept alive with them.

The residual shock from the pyramid—that I might have been responsible for the death of something as big and beautiful as a horse—was profound. I experienced nightmares for a long time, imagining a horse's head was severed or a horse's body suddenly appearing in a dumpster. I was the culprit in these dreams, just like the media decreed. In each dream, I would panic and try to cover any trace of the act, hide the

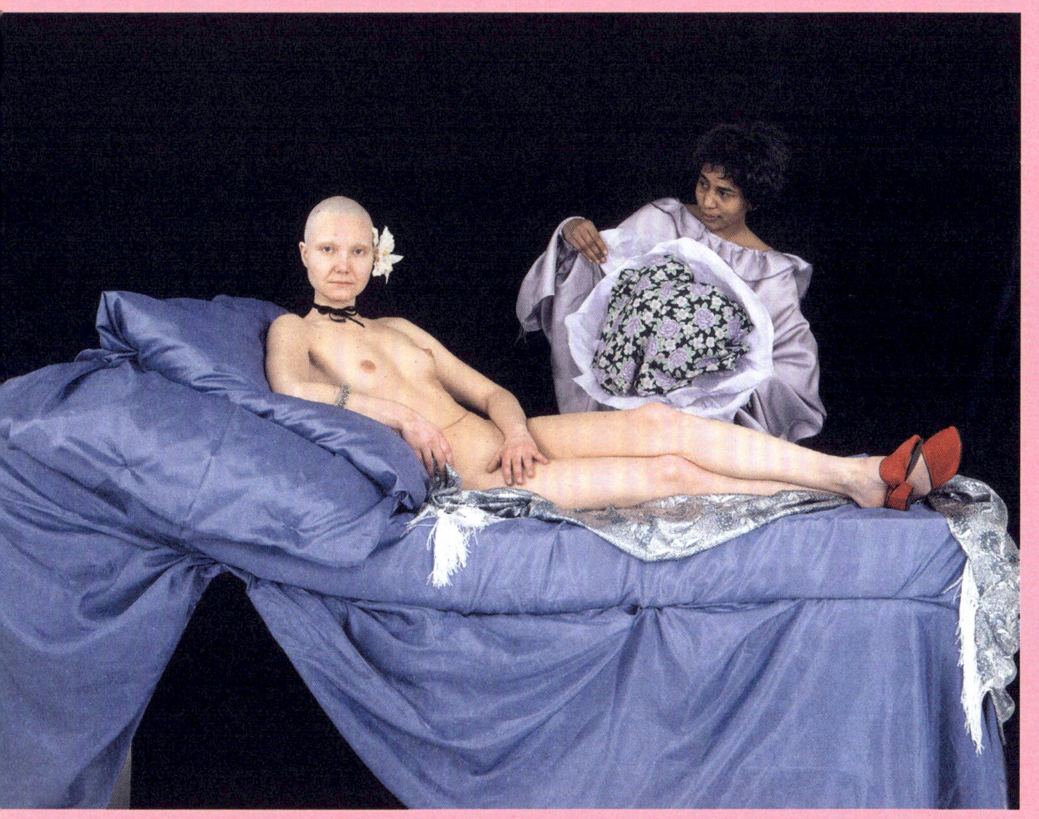

Olympia, 1996

corpus delicti that might point to me as the person responsible for the giant corpse.

Have you dreamed about other work?

Only this one. Sometimes it was a horse carcass with no skin. Sometimes it was a human. The carcass either had no head or it was a head with no body. Sometimes the setting was a hospital or a morgue. I dreamed that the space consisted of a tiled room in which there was no bed, only an operating table.

As long as slaughter takes place anonymously and individuals remain anonymous within a society of consumers and carnivores, there is a kind of peace. Everything is meant to be impersonal and anonymity means no one is to blame. Consumption is normal as long as no individual is in charge. In this structure, anything can happen. But if you dare to give up your anonymity, madness ensues. One is expelled from society. *(pauses)*

Something tragic happened with the *Olympia* story: my young friend died in hospital, aged 19.

How did you make the decision to exhibit her in both video and photos?

The most important thing for me was the video. It comes from a time in which I didn't know how to present myself as a young sick person or otherwise. I also questioned what kind of woman I was—what kind of creature.

Your interest in the body courses through many works, including *Rite of Spring*.

Yes. My preoccupation with choreography and semi-theatrical forms is related to my interest in the body, identity, and the possibilities of movement. With *Rite of Spring*, I found myself intrigued by the question of how to animate a choreography that one cannot know, in this case, because Nijinsky's performances were not filmed in the early twentieth century.

It was a formative experience to discover firsthand what was so awkward about Nijinsky's original movements. He negated everything that dancers had been taught, and what amazed me in particular was how he managed to choreograph against his dancers' best habits and the intuitive balance of their bodies.

Nijinsky's *Sacrificial Dance* should really be performed to a point of complete exhaustion. I was fascinated by his jerky, contorted movements. At that time, I was still photographing old people and so the combination of age and dancing to a point of death became my guiding concept. I also found it

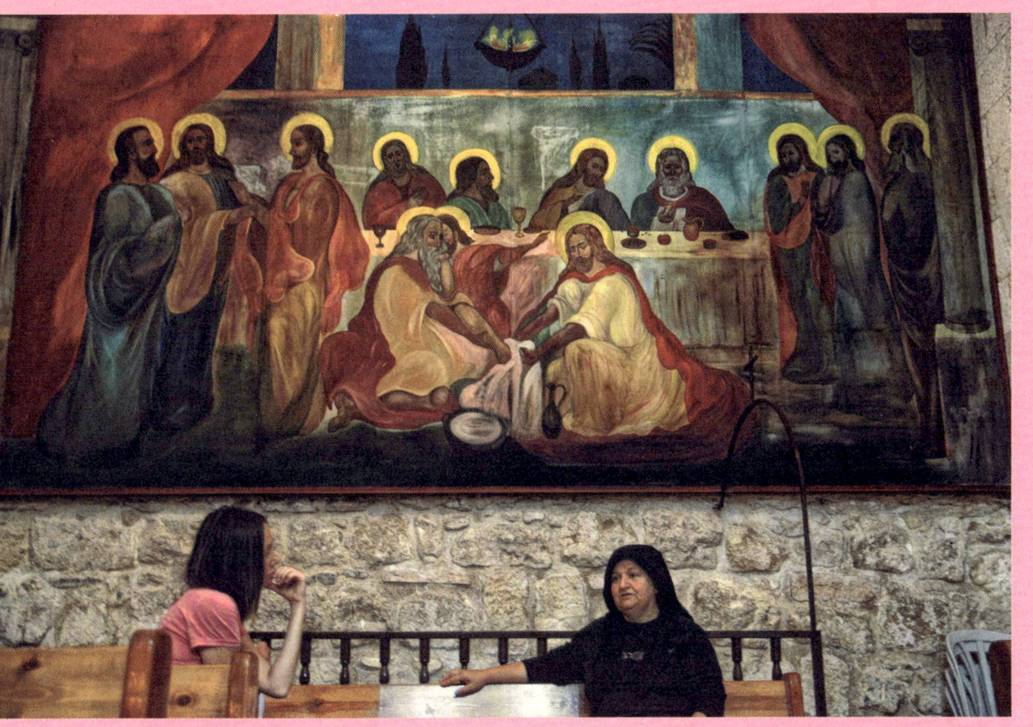

Looking for Jesus, 2013–

interesting to imagine a dance that an old person could never actually do. I wanted to show that the body is a costume.

Like Michelangelo painted in his *Last Judgment*.

Yes, the body as a suit. The figures in my video are naked and male and female sexual organs and gender attributes are swapped. I connected idea with process and had little trouble realizing and shooting the first thirty seconds, but by the time I got to minute four, I couldn't work anymore.

What do you mean?

I didn't have a template like [Marie-Claude] Pietragalla had and so I didn't know how to further reconstruct Nijinsky's choreography. Pietragalla filmed from one point of view, with dancers moving on a single line, so her impression was straight on, flat and two-dimensional. I realized I had to shift from making a film to an animation. After a long time discussing the problem with specialists, we came up with the idea of hiring a single ballet dancer who would learn the choreography step by step and dance it for me. I realized I needed my own template so that I could translate it into an animation that would then become my *Rite of Spring*.

In *Looking for Jesus* (2013–) you once again walk a line between performance and reality.

Yes. My interest in *Looking for Jesus* was to see what difference it makes when a person doesn't pretend to be Jesus or the Messiah, but really believes they are him. I was interested in people who are in what they call "direct contact" with—I don't know what to call it—God. I wanted to look for someone like that and find out if there was a person who was so convincing that I believed them.

How did you start this project?

Well, the idea continues to develop. I let myself be influenced by the people I talk to. I eliminate what is too far away from what interests me and take into consideration anything else that somehow fits into this initial framework.

And in between you find a form?

Every subject needs its own form. *Looking for Jesus* is the first time I've dealt with text. In it, language comes first. The core of the work is what people say rather than what they do or how they look. The video provides visual accompaniment and I have never really done anything similar, in that sense.

Video usually provides the core of my artistic statements. This work marks the first time that there are so many distinct people who have informed the project, through interviews. I have to interview people long enough for something interesting to come out and that can be really challenging. Each time I had to adjust to a new person, because all the things I learned along the way—what kind of questions I ask and how I react to answers—often did not fit other subjects. They even at times, disturb them.

I imagine that these people in particular are driven by a strong sense of self.

Absolutely, but I actually like to subordinate my own ego amidst these kinds of characters. No other way! As a counter example, when I was developing my *Faces* project (2004–06), I could hardly stand the dancers. That was a different kind of ego.

In what way?

I found the egos of those dancers very limiting. In my experience, dancers are trained to understand their dances within a particular structure, from beginning to end, and that structure is in a sense closed. The dance exists in a way that means its dancer is always subordinate. When dancers are dealing with someone who comes from a different division of power or structure, they snap and disrespect that other. I could have done with help from a respected choreographer, someone in the field who the dancers might have recognized and listened to a bit more. With the "Jesus" figures it was different. I quite appreciated their egos and the speakers themselves were happy that at last someone was listening *(laughs)*. I was someone who brought an audience with me! Those kinds of difficult characters are very close to me.

Is a viewer meant to sense that when watching the video?

No, I don't think so. The closeness happened over time, as I learned to understand each individual. I wanted the video to be true to its genesis, so that the relationships appear as I experienced them at the time, starting with early encounters. I also really liked Jerusalem's electric atmosphere. The city's energy appealed to me. I am used to tension and even need it, I think.

Do you find it here in Warsaw?

No, here I feel I am in a neutral place. I feel at home in the actual space I inhabit, but I don't really feel it in Warsaw itself.

When I first came face to face with Julie Mehretu's work at the Berlin gallery Carlier | Gebauer in 2004, I was overwhelmed, practically thunderstruck. Having never seen anything by her before, I was taken aback by the complexity of the paintings, by their dynamic compositions. At that moment, I could not have imagined more appealing work.

Purely by chance, I bumped into Friedrich Meschede, then the director of DAAD, at the opening, in front of a painting grounded by a central perspective that made us both think of Albrecht Altdorfer's *Alexanderschlacht* (The Battle of Alexander at Issus, 1529)—an iconic piece we knew from Munich's Alte Pinakothek. Chaotic turmoil in an overarching structure, strong colors, stormy energy, forces pushing toward the center from all sides in an open field: I found all of this, albeit abstract and on a light background that looked as if it had been polished smooth, once again in Mehretu's *Congress*, from 2003. Even the position of certain marks like pennants, and a particular sign which appears in the center, on the top part of both paintings, conjured Altdorfer's work.

In this exhibition, however, probably because of my preference for asymmetry, I liked *Manifestation* (2003) most of all. Here too, bold red lines of energy roamed freely rather than purposefully over an endlessly layered landscape without a horizon. An accumulation of strokes, dots, and squiggles suggest vegetation; watery blue and gray areas suggest ponds or air currents, cloud banks or veils of mist in motion. If *Congress* makes me think of the combination of forces that collide at political demonstrations, then *Manifestation* pulls my imagination towards cosmic or atmospheric phenomena. Without a clear perspective, everything appears to exist in a kind of specific limbo, similar to El Lissitzky's *Proun* from the 1920s. Unlike Lissitzky's, however, Mehretu's work is not about three-dimensional bodies that glide weightlessly through space. Instead, she renders pictorial space with both arrow-straight and curved lines that sweep across myriad, translucent layers, and populates it with architectural structures or abbreviations.

I think in her masterfully organized, paradoxical combination of order and chaos I find something reminiscent of Wassily Kandinsky, and in her fleet-footed drawings of lines, perhaps some inspiration from Leonardo da Vinci. One could very easily continue to enumerate how sovereignly Julie Mehretu wields the history of painting to create new images above all these layers, well beyond mere quotation or illustration, to reflect what she herself experiences and which are thus indicative and evocative of the experiences of her generation and the revolutionary changes in her, in our, present. *As told to Isabel Parkes*

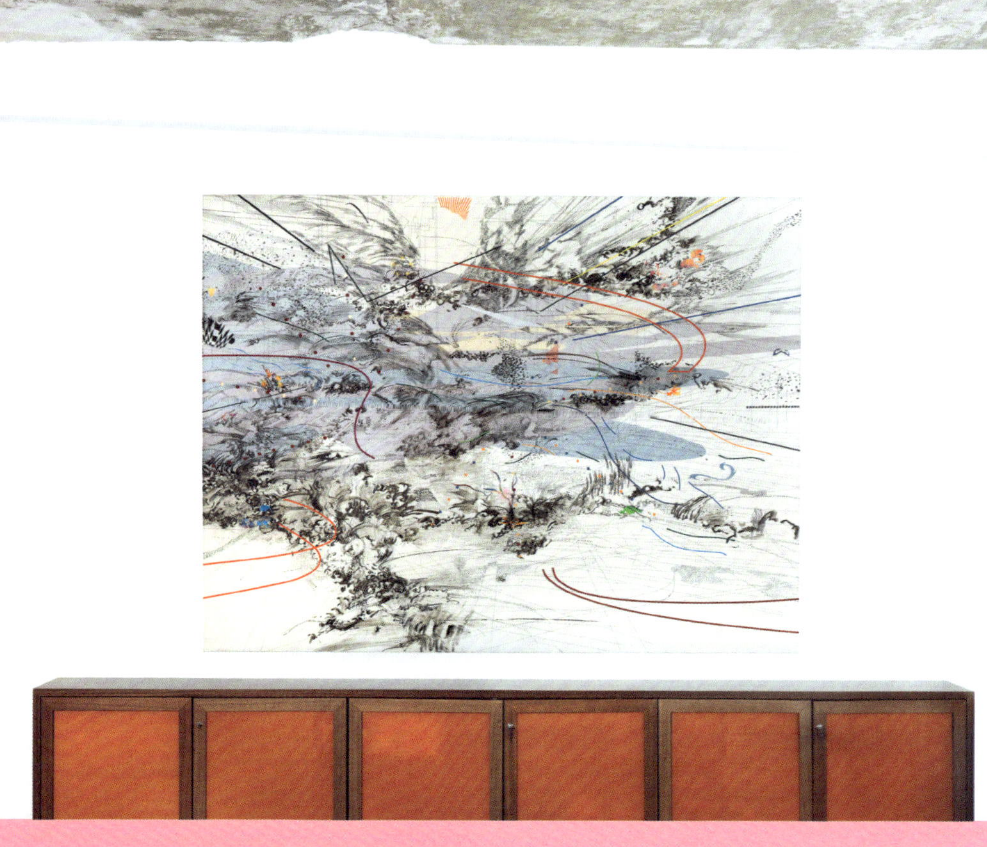

Manifestation, 2003
Sammlung Hoffmann Installation XVIII, 2014–15

Language and titles feel central to your practice. Where do you begin before you go to canvas?

There are many different points of entry for me with any given painting or group of paintings, and I like to I think of them as moments in which I'm working. Of course, my relationship with work and with myself changes over time, so the way I titled work when I was younger differs from how I title work today. That said, titles continue to operate as another layer of information, rather than a description. I don't use text in my paintings, so the title-as-text offers another sense of direction. Sometimes the title comes from the way a word looks next to the way the painting looks; sometimes it comes from how the word sounds or how the title sounds next to how it looks; sometimes it is a specific location that's immersed in the painting; other times, it comes from a text I've read.

I'm struck to hear you consider the way the word looks, because a key element in your work is line, which is equally part of writing. What does the line offer you?

The line is among the most rudimentary forms of a mark. My earliest paintings came from me taking apart the way I approached mark-making: taking it down to the level of individual marks as glyphs and then trying to understand different glyphs' meanings. Making marks offers a way to invent a new language. Using marks as a form of self-referential language and gesture led me to lines.

Can you describe the process of starting a painting with no particular reference in mind?

It is rare for me to start a painting with no particular reference in mind. I usually have some sort of point of entry that conceptually helps determine the paintings or bodies of work. Often, starting with a preconceived vision for a painting undermines what it can be. I rely hugely on intuition in terms of how I move forward with images.

A friend of mine once said that he tries to speak before he thinks, and I try to work in a place for that to happen. In many ways, I feel that what the work is doing and what my hands are doing within the work are ahead of where my head is, in terms of understanding. This gap is where the most interesting shifts take place.

This is also how I came to start using more architectural language in my work: it was an intuitive gesture that informed the work in terms of social space and time. Then it became an investigation of trying to understand exactly that. There is a process of trying to make sense of what's happening or what's taking place in the work. One can't make from a place of trying to make sense, one makes from somewhere else, and then perhaps one can interpret, or come to better understand oneself.

This feels related to earlier conversations about abstract versus representational work

I think that the most interesting representational work calls into question what it represents. I work within the language of abstraction because it allows me to work things out that I couldn't otherwise, but there are moments of representation there.

I imagine a real awareness of both. That you're so conscious of this connection that you become unaware of the significance of decisions related to it—

Yes, and there are moments within abstraction where you can see an image. Likewise, you can get lost in abstract gestures in areas that feel very representational. The abstraction-figuration binary is a fictive construct.

I once encountered your work in the Sammlung Hoffmann next to a *Proun* (ca. 1920) by El Lissitzky. It was adjacent to a room filled with work by Frank Stella. I imagine both artists work similarly to how you describe your own experience of this fictive opposition.

Intuition is a place for different forms of connectedness, a way of being driven and of trying to make sense of language, but also allowing a new possibility to take place within a broader language. I don't think one can explicitly invent a new form of language. Everything I'm using—every mark—is part of a language that has been understood and worked with before. You bring up two artists who have very much informed my process, but there are many others who haven't left any mark, printed or drawn, but who have been super formative for me. Mine is a constant recalling of language and forms of making, and at the same time looking for a fissure or break with them. It's mining for a place where something else can emerge.

Can you name some of the others?

So many and such a range! David Hammons *(pauses)*. Kara Walker, Tacita Dean, Frank Stella, who you mentioned. In fact, the huge *Moby Dick* piece [*Of Whales in Paint; in Teeth; in Wood...*, 1990] that Erika owns has such a presence for me. I remember being at several Artemis Quartet concerts at their house, looking at the piece and seeing it change. The more time you spend with it, the more it changes.

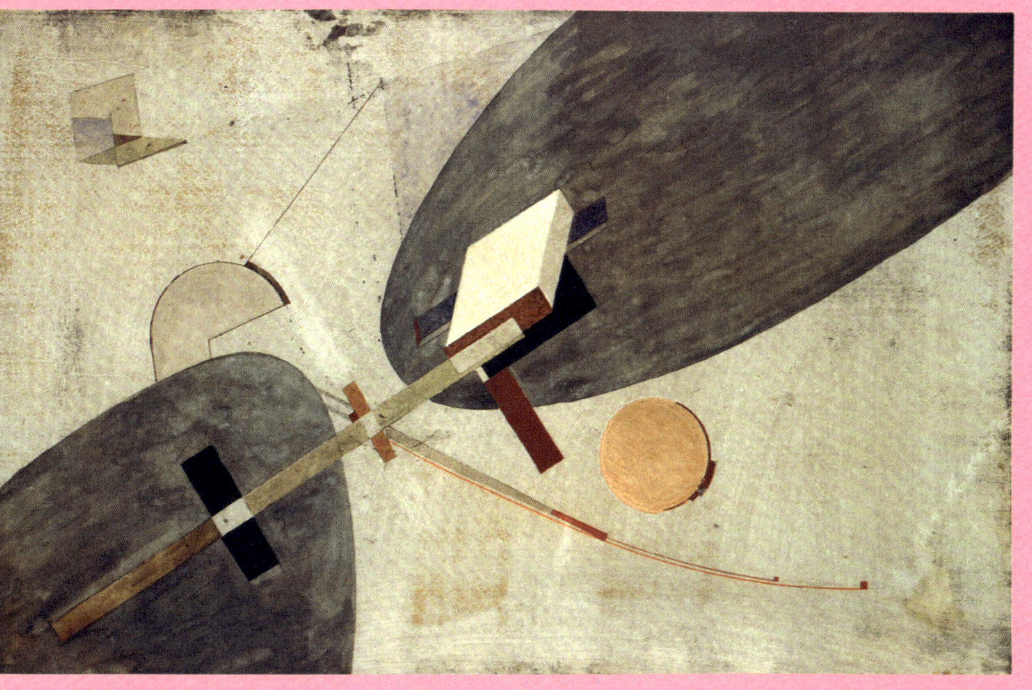

El Lissitzky, *Proun*, ca. 1920

I think about that a lot: about the time-based experience of painting. I think about it with my own work but it's also something that I think of as important in the general experience of painting. A lot of people have forgotten that way of looking. I think in this moment—where we have a lot of new media and work that is itself a timed experience—that the way people consume images is continually shifting. In addition, of course, to social media and how quickly and we consume a massive number of images. Paintings are made on a different timescale and require attentive, long periods of looking in order to be activated. I've really had that kind of time-based experience at Erika's with that particular Stella piece. I think a lot of people have.

When did you meet Erika?

I think the first time I met Erika was at their home, when she was hosting the annual reopening of the collection. It was incredible to experience such an immense array of work so seriously considered in a single installation.

Do you find that a time-based experience of art relates to scale?

Scale is part of it, but you can also have that experience with small paintings. I can think of Richard Tuttle paintings that are so tiny and that demand you spend time with them in order to understand their logic and rhythm. I don't know that size is a determining aspect of experience.

You've spoken previously about a professor at the Rhode Island School of Design who would talk to you about who you were as a person. This feels connected to your journey to develop a practice bound to your own experiences.

As a teacher, Michael Young would spend time getting to know you and understanding who you were before he tried to make sense of the work. He wasn't trying to understand what was going on in your studio. He wanted to get to know you, and for you to know him. Little by little, things would come up in conversation in terms of works, but always more directed by who you were.

This definitely informed my approach to working: I looked to myself to make sense of what I was trying to do. I still use that approach as a guiding principle to make sense of who I am in a moment, and in turn what I'm doing with the work.

How do you, how does any artist, protect herself within a creative process that can be so personal and demanding?

The work I make comes from a particular part of me, propelled by a generative momentum of the creative practice. My relationship to my work expresses an evolution similar to how I, how one, develops as a person. The two are inextricable.

It's practically become a cliché when talking about your work, but an experience of globalization feels present in many of the pieces in the Sammlung Hoffmann. Do you still feel it's a relevant point to understanding both your person and your work?

I think there are moments in which what certain artists are doing seems to align with and depict a specific moment in time, and I certainly think that some of my paintings touch on particular dynamics that defined the end of the twentieth century. The speed with which events around the world were taking place and continue to take place is something that has shifted and shaped all of us. Those of us who were born elsewhere or raised in a time that preceded globalization have a very different understanding of the world from those who grew up with, say, a unified Europe. It's similar for friends who have grown up in an Africa in which you could only get certain goods if a relative flew from abroad and brought that thing home with them. You couldn't find everything, everywhere. Today, nobody brings you back the pot from Italy that you can just as easily get at Williams-Sonoma. We are in a different moment.

When you've experienced both moments, you are informed by both. What was taking place in my earlier works was really an investigation of marks and place and visual language. I don't see the paintings as descriptive of myself, in that sense. I think they were more engaged with an evolving language and figuring out who I was as I negotiated that language, and why.

I think one can understand that in the case of *Heavy Weather* (2005) in the Sammlung Hoffmann. I remember a visitor asking me about Hurricane Katrina while looking at those prints.

I didn't think about Katrina when I made those. Storms, in the sense of life change, were part of the landscape I lived in at the time. I was working at Crown Point Press in San Francisco and had been staying in a hotel that housed some families who were on assistance because they had lost their New Orleans homes. At the time, I also had a new child, my partner and I had just moved into a new home, and Katrina came and what it exposed really shifted political discourse in the United States. This was the broader landscape I inhabited. I was working on that particular group of works and the title became *Heavy Weather*, not in direct relation to Katrina. It was later that I realized the connection—and that's what I mean when I talk about intuition being more synchronized with a relationship to the world than to the rational mind. There's a lot that informs my work, and as a person, I find myself frequently playing catch up.

It's interesting to think about the process of interpretation here: what viewers see

It's part of the process of abstraction. What can be frustrating is when people deny the chance to understand what is possible in the work or try to hold an artist in a specific place. Artists get pigeonholed constantly. Stella is a phenomenal example of refusing that, and I don't mean refusing with statements. He has refused with his work. Personally, I feel the span of time that I've been making work is still quite short in relation to my recognized process. As a creative person, you often don't have a choice to refuse certain aspects of being held down.

What does refusal look like in your practice?

Refusal comes from insisting on change in both the work and in one's own person. Refusal is exorcising or silencing the critics as well as the acclaim.

We encountered the first soft sculptures by Ernesto Neto while visiting Rosa and Carlos de la Cruz in Miami. We walked into their place and saw a few light-hued, round bags on the floor. Rosa lifted up one after the other and *plop!*—as they fell, they each created a specific shape. At the time, we couldn't find any publications about the artist, but Rosa photocopied a newspaper article for us in which the New York gallery Bonakdar Jancou was mentioned. Once we were back in New York, we visited Marc Jancou, who, with the help of photos, devoted himself to introducing us to Ernesto Neto's seductive work. Though we were enthralled, we were hesitant to acquire one of his colorful room installations. But we didn't forget those images.

In June 1998, at Art Basel—a fair we visited annually, starting in 1980, because we felt it was where we could consistently see the most interesting work—we were very much drawn to Ernesto Neto's white room installation, which was delicately scented by pepper and nutmeg. It was while speaking with the charismatic Marcantonio Vilaça from São Paulo that we became fully convinced, and together we agreed that the artist would install the work himself in our home. Next thing we knew, there he was: Ernesto Neto standing in front of our door in July 1998, weighed down by a giant rucksack that concealed his "egg," filled with little polystyrene balls, and a travel sack with the other components: paper-thin Lycra and bags with ground pepper and nutmeg. We met a charming young man.

Later on, Ernesto told me how his gallerist had really made a point of explaining to him how he must behave with collectors. In any case, he was indeed amiable, punctual, very well organized, and a skillful improviser; it was a real pleasure to work with him. When I showed him the room that I had in mind for his work, he convinced me in a friendly kind of way that his *Nave Óvulo Organóide* (1998) would actually have a much better effect in a larger space. And so, we changed our plans and transformed the set-up according to his suggestion. Ernesto found tools in our kitchen and got some from the janitor, but otherwise made do with what he had. And when he wanted to adapt his *Nave* to our particular spatial situation, he put my sewing machine on a piece of board, propped up between two ladders, and, standing, began to sew with an immeasurable amount of fabric at his feet. Before determining final positions or making finishing touches, he would always lie down on one of the worktables or inside his *Nave* and close his eyes for twenty minutes.

As Ernesto stayed with us over the years, he and Rolf enjoyed long conversations, and they came to have an especially close bond. This closeness to Rolf is something that Ernesto also extended to me. Even if we don't write to each other for a year because doing so in English is not particularly satisfying to either of us, when we do have the chance meet each other in person again, the encounter is heartfelt. *As told to Isabel Parkes*

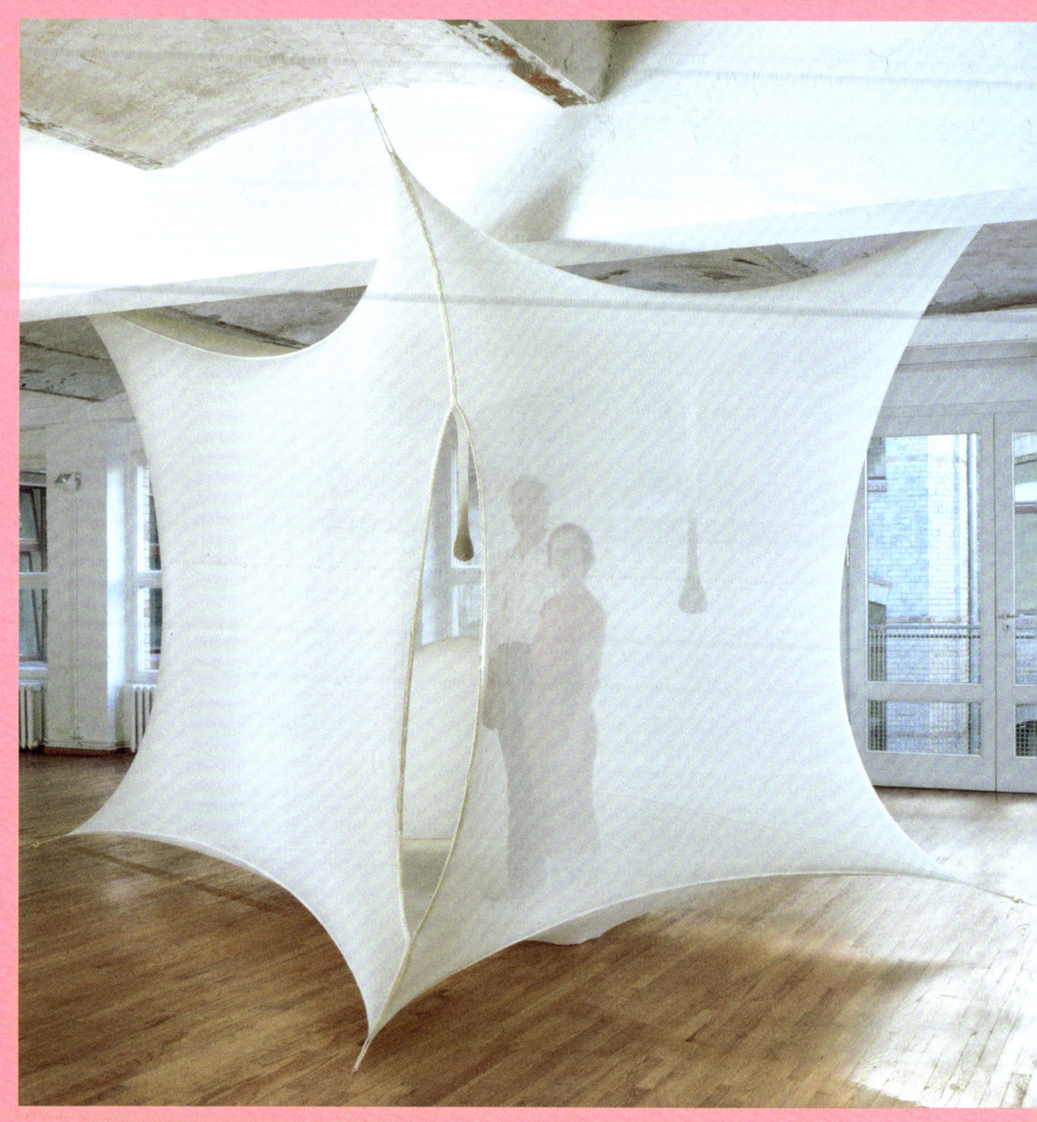

Nave Óvulo Organóide, 1998
Sammlung Hoffmann Installation II, 1998–99

You want me to tell a story?

Please!

I think Erika and Rolf heard about me through Rosa and Carlos de la Cruz in Miami, but they first encountered my work in Basel in 1998, when Galeria Camargo Vilaça, renamed Fortes Vilaça after Marcantonio Vilaça's passing, and today known as Fortes D'Aloia & Gabriel, took part for the first time. Marcantonio showed *The sky is the anatomy of my body* (1988) and, after meeting Erika and Rolf, was very excited to tell me that they were interested in the *Nave* I was working on at that time.

That piece, *Nave Óvulo Organóide* (1998) was made with two spice drops and one ovaloid form. I remember folding the textiles into my bag, a trick I borrowed from the *camelô* or Brazilian street sellers to make things easy to transport and temporarily build. The ovaloid was full of polystyrene, light but big, so I covered it with cardboard and tape, and carried it. I remember flying overnight and not sleeping much, landing in Paris, and finally emerging at Tegel Airport with a big egg on my trolley, taller than me. When I arrived at their home, Erika took me to the kitchen to make some food and we began to talk nonstop. A year later, they acquired another work, *Paff Paff Puff, Puff Puff Puff Paff* (1999) and again, I came to Berlin to install the work in their home. I remember going with Rolf to a warehouse far on the other side of the city to buy bulk spices.

What did Berlin feel like at the time?

Like another world! I had actually been there a few years before and found it, especially Mitte, fascinating. There were bars playing new electronic music and videos, buildings inhabited only by artists, incredible energy that vibrated with the trams, through the river and parks. Already on my second trip, I found Mitte more domesticated, but it was then that Erika, Rolf and I really explored the city together by car. Rolf wanted to show me how everything was being rebuilt. I could feel the explosion of culture as he talked to me, a Carioca beach boy, listening in silence and taking it in. I sensed communication between a messy Berlin and a messy Rio, and I remember thinking in terms of the relationship between the figure and the background: in Europe, the relation between the figure and the background is clear and defined with sharp lines. In Brazil, the forest sits between the figure and the background, and from there, anything can happen.

What was Brazil like for you at that time?

I was living in my studio, which we called *atelienave*, a downtown, three-story building that is still not quite in the center. I come from southern Rio, which is considered the picture-perfect part between the mountains and open-armed Christ, with Copacabana, Ipanema, and Leblon beaches in between and a lake in the center. At that time in my life, I was moving from one girlfriend, very dense and filled with spice, to another much more ethereal, called Lili, with whom I now share two kids. In a way, this shift represents a passage for me from puffs and paffs, to the skies and naves. I had just enjoyed an incredible summer, during which we—a group of friends from the beach—were inventing things, dancing, singing, and making parties everywhere we could. I began to date Lili just before this Basel fair and meeting the Hoffmanns.

Has installing in private homes changed your work?

As far as I can remember, I have only installed my work in Rosa and Carlos de la Cruz's home and Erika and Rolf's. I don't know if the process itself changed the work, but close encounters with these people have been very important. The notion of a home as a uterine and cave-like space has always felt central to me and for a long time, my studio was my bedroom. I like to work, feel, think, and dream on the bed, and to draw with paper on the floor, with my belly resting on the mattress. This sense of intimacy allows me to create a strong home ambiance, so generally I would say going into someone else's feels familiar.

Tell me about starting to work with gallerist Tanya Bonakdar.
It seems like an energetic moment for you.

Yes, Tanya was a friend of Marcia Fortes, who also had work of mine in her home. Tanya had visited Miami to see a show called *Defining the Nineties* about young artists represented in collections in Miami, NY, and LA, and there, she encountered my work. In July 1996, I had an exhibition in Chicago, and after that, I flew to New York to meet with Tanya. I was again carrying a work with me and Tanya had a summer show up. She spontaneously invited me to include the work, so I did.

The moment itself was creative and there was real attention on what we as artists were doing. Young people still lived in Soho and I think many people in New York felt like they were "discovering" Latin America. They did not necessarily know our Brazilian environment, but we knew their culture, and it felt like we could offer joy and freshness and life. Curators also began to arrive in my studio in Rio. My work at that time was different from what was going on around me and had a strong relationship to Brazilian art history, to *neoconcretismo* and artists like [Lygia] Clark, [Lygia] Pape, Hélio [Oiticica], Tunga,

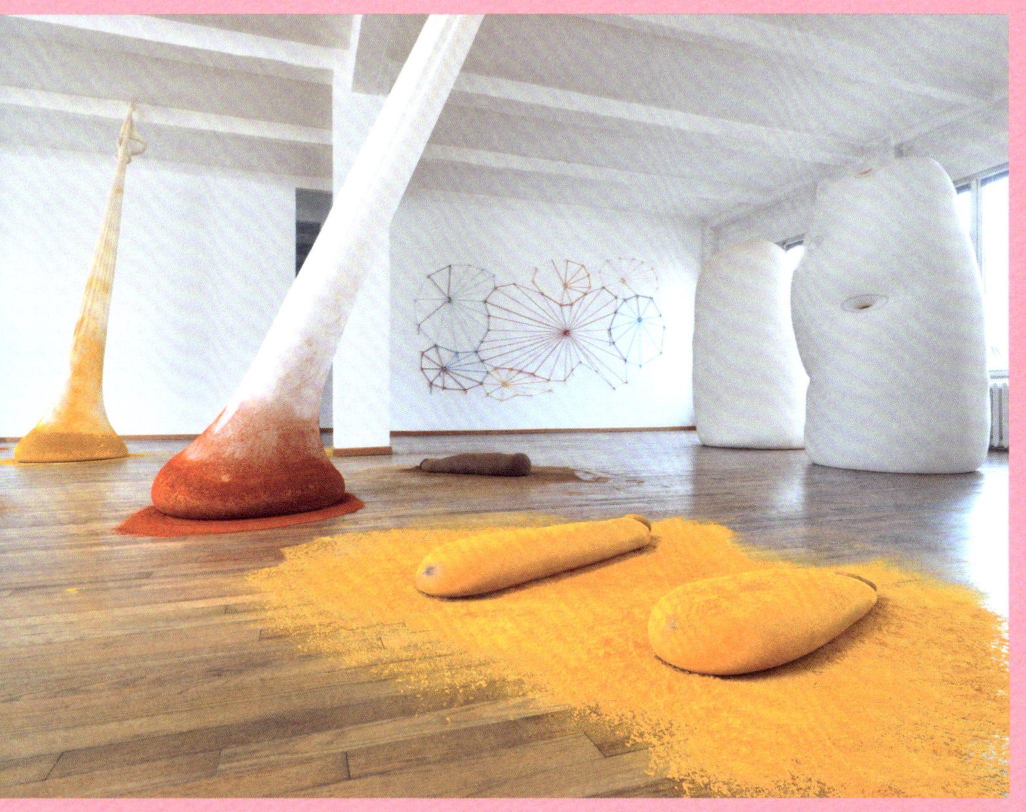

paff puff and the eternal infinite, 1998
Untitled (Dry Color Field), 2005
Follicle Ovaloid (Pete), 1998
Follicle Ovaloid (Lili), 1998
Sammlung Hoffmann Installation XIV, 2010–11

[Artur] Barrio, Waltercio [Caldas], Cildo [Meireles]. Europe was beginning to unify, and it was looking at itself. Under all these circumstances my work began to be seen, and Tanya saw it.

What about your work do you think initially attracted attention?

I think to certain people, I expressed a Brazilian spirit and something of Brazilian history. The way we understand the world in Brazil comes through digging, through finding things, maybe because we have to constantly improvise and because information is, or certainly was not, available everywhere. As a place, Brazil is more focused on the individual than the institutional. Not in an individualist sense, but in the sense of finding solutions independently. At the same time, there is a collective energy that reaches beyond our failing institutions, and this energy gives us freedom but little support.

Can you say more about those historical influences?

At the end of the 1950s, the government was building Brasilia. When they finished building Brasilia, there was no place in it for the people who had worked there. At the same time as you have what one might call the social contract in Brazil, you have the worker, who makes *samba*. While to some, this is a second or third class of work, this kind of worker has poetry, dance, singing, music, art, and community. Someone like this had a formally "bad" job but is within an informal society from which ultimately the most important event in Rio de Janeiro has arisen. *Carnaval* represents a utopia of people working together. When you are not formally part of a social contract, the only thing you have is your own body, your own subjectivity. From this you can generate a counter-cultural environment. And this is an institution in itself: a counter-cultural institution, in which many can create dances and environments.

The artists of *Neoconcretismo* felt all this and began to work with the reality of body relations. They felt and perceived what was not part of so-called social democratic thinking of the time, for example what was beneath Brasilia. When *Concretismo* shifted to *Neoconcretismo*, it was political and historic. Those partaking did not explicitly understand it this way, but they were somehow acknowledging a lack. I believe that we Brazilians are body people. *Paff Paff Puff, Puff Puff Puff Paff* is a work made with and for a body in close conversation with landscape. When you "paff" a work it is as if the energy flows out of your body and into the landscape. I want people in my work to feel like they are alive and know that they are made up of many cells.

Colônia (1988) captures this.

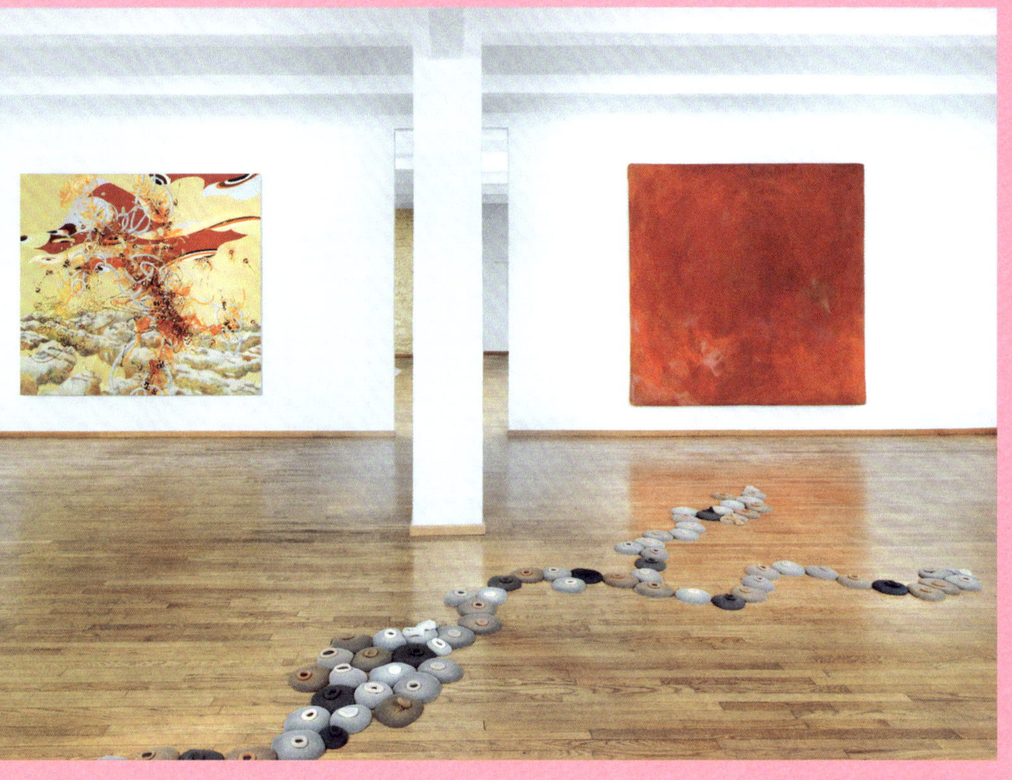

Ernesto Neto, *Colônia*, 1988
Matthew Ritchie, *A Glorious Martyrdom Awaits Us All at the Hands of Our Tender and Merciful God*, 2003
Gotthard Graubner, *Brazen Snake*, 1985
Sammlung Hoffmann Installation XVII, 2013–14

Yes! *Colônia* is a kind of metaphor for the cells inside of us. Every time I install it, it requires a code, and yet every time, I have to remake the code. I recently did so in Basel, which was different than the version Erika has, made first in 1988. I am different today, of course, but the piece also teaches me. It's a dance every time I make it. *(pauses)* In many ways, that work was the seed of everything for me. It was my rupture from the mechanical to the organic. I was making a lot around age thirty. Between thirty and forty is when we express who we are. Later, we expand. Before, we invent.

The specificity of cells as in- or outside of the body seems largely irrelevant to your work, which often exists between states.

You know, the Olmec heads were found covered with plants in the middle of the Mexican jungle. Nature is full and if you consider the most commonly accepted idea of space, it is the idea of the void. You don't imagine a landscape that puts you in the middle of the jungle, but this is the kind of landscape that I know best.

You build a house in Brazil and then a tree begins to grow, and it breaks your side wall. We have a situation that is the opposite of many societies in the north, where you don't find this power of nature, this excess of life. There is too much life here, too many energies happening at the same time. We think that culture is independent of nature–oh my sister!–I know culture as an extension of nature. All the material, the chemical, the spiritual, the physical parts of my works we have talked about, they come from nature. We are just the ones who bring these parts together for processing.

The reality is that contemporary space is full and it is here, too *(touching stomach)*. The systems, the cells, the urban networks of roads and cars, these are organic, these are space and body. If you think about my early works in Erika and Rolf's home, you see they are much more about internal mass density and about gaining connection to the earth. The *Naves* and the *Ovaloids* open to space, to *this* space. Even the *Nave* holds air, showing us that we are not in a void and that air is matter.

Can you speak to the significance of play in your work?

This has become very important in the times in which we live. When you think about how we cannot touch most art, the issue is mostly conservation. You cannot touch what must exist forever.

And also because of perceived value.

Ah, well now we are talking about the subject! In the world we experience, this is becoming more important than even our relationship with other people. People do not touch themselves or each other, because they could develop a problem. There is a huge evolution of untouchable situations, this sense of clean, and this so-called orientation towards the future, of all things. Everything is so clean, so bare. You see a plaza and it is spotless, and then you notice a tree there and that tree actually looks dirty. Nature is becoming dirty to human beings: "I don't want to sit here in this earth, I could get dirty!" or, "There are ants on the grass!" At the end of the day, we are the dirt. We shit, we pee. I mean, I love to shower, to get clean. But I also love to be warm, sweaty, feel this porosity of the body. Many of my recent pieces have been highly interactive and in or around them, people talk to each other because they find, feel themselves in an unexpected situation.

What do you think surprise does?

It is so important to take people out of the established moment in which they are living. I believe that most of the answers to uncertainties and questions are inside of us. We are used to a situation in which politicians, religions, artists, writers, teachers, and various others say things that influence society. People constantly tell others what to do. What if instead we could create the conditions that help people find answers for themselves? I mean within their relationships, the places they live, or through artwork. Maybe the work itself can stimulate something inside of people that generates the possibility of discovering answers on one's own.

I recall a remark made by Jan Hoet in Cologne during one of the many talks he gave while preparing for documenta IX, in 1992: Hoet wanted the artist to penetrate reality as it presents itself to us, to move through the world, and in so doing, depart from it.

Other artists of Albert Oehlen's generation also connected this "moving through" to a persistent questioning of the worlds around them. Through dismantling and dovetailing, layers and reflections, Oehlen developed his own approach to images that the world has offered him. We got to know him, as well as [Werner] Büttner, [Georg] Herold and [Martin] Kippenberger, at Max Hetzler's gallery, who had just moved from Stuttgart to Cologne when we arrived there.

Albert Oehlen interested us as someone who seemed to still believe in painting or at least used painting, which was a medium in which we ourselves actually no longer believed. We had been raised on the idea that painting could no longer bring forth anything new, that although it was rich in tradition, it was out of touch with the present day, simply outdated. Oehlen grappled with painting and that notion. His work clearly reflects the conflicts one experiences in the process of painting. He seems to constantly be pushing back against the possibilities of the medium, to be acting as if he can't paint at all. His painting is never carried out to completion, no image is what one might call "totally painted." In his paintings, there are not only disruptions, but also injuries. We found—and I still find—it interesting that he completes a process only to reverse it, that he turns pictures while he's working on them, that he allows the paint to run or drip, that he demonstrates and lays bare both technical mistakes and apparent clumsiness. To this day, I find surprises every time I look at his paintings, and this makes me want to look much more closely. Yet I also believe that I have never understood Oehlen's approach! This adds to my fascination.

The idea that one can learn everything about a picture simply by looking closely often hindered me from asking artists or gallerists questions. It was first with Americans that I dared to ask anything. Today, you'll find German artists who like to talk about—are even quite forthcoming about—their work, but in the past, they would be offended or turn away if you wanted to know, let alone ask, something.

Is there such a thing as correct understanding? Wanting to understand is of course personal, and what you see and feel cannot ever truly be put into words. At most, you might attempt to get closer to a work, but this closeness cannot fundamentally be transferred to a different medium or mode of expression. What interests me so much in this regard is the exchange of ideas: that I could be standing in front of the same thing as you and we might never be sure that we see the same image.
As told to Isabel Parkes

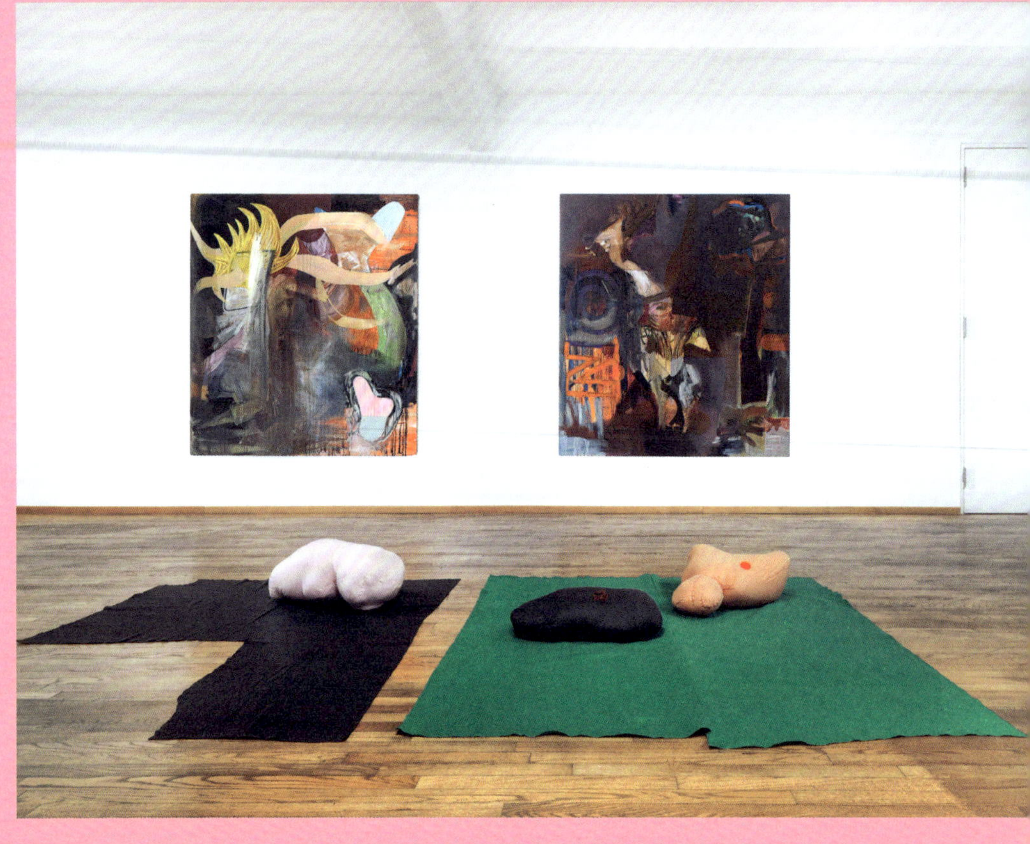

Mike Kelley, *Figure/Ground*, 1990
Albert Oehlen, *FN 29*, 1990
Albert Oehlen, *FN Romantic*, 1990
Sammlung Hoffmann Installation XVIII, 2014–15

How big is your studio in Switzerland?

About 150 square meters.

Do you paint multiple pictures at the same time?

Three or four, so that they can dry.

Do you mix colors on a palette?

Never on a palette, always on the canvas.

Where does the paint come from?

From a tube.

Do you use gloves?

No, I try to stay clean.

Do you manage?

If the studio is clean, yes. If it's disorganized and nothing's been moved around for too long—and by that I mean my palette as well—then I start to get pretty filthy. I really don't like getting covered in paint. I don't like the smell either.

Does it give you a headache?

No, I'm too used to it.

Do you work with assistants?

Rarely. Well, I don't have permanent ones. Sometimes, when I have a lot to do and I know what needs to be done, friends come to visit for a few days and then we work on things together. I'm always happy about the change in atmosphere. They're all artists themselves.

Do you talk when you're in the studio together?

Of course!

Do you listen to music?

Yes, and sometimes radio.

Do you have a sofa in your studio?

Unfortunately.

Do you have an archive of references?

I used to have one. I still have it, but I don't use it anymore, although I might need it again someday, so I haven't thrown it away.

Do you take photos?

Almost never.

I noticed yesterday that I have 10,000 photos on my phone.

I've got thirty.

Seeing with a mobile phone changes one's view.

Sure, but photos don't matter to me.

What are you looking at these days?

I don't look at anything. My reference is always the previous work. The idea comes from the work.

How do you start a painting?

I set myself a specific task.

Do you currently have specific parameters that are informing your work, in other words, conditions you are relying on?

Not at the moment actually, because I've just recently completed a body of work for the Serpentine in London. I don't know what I'm going to do next.

Perhaps then we can talk about a specific work, like *Mill by Moonlight* (1999).

Yes, that's from a series called the gray paintings, which had certain guidelines according to which the works were made. But now the problem is that I've already told this story one hundred times. Sorry.

You mentioned earlier that at the time, the idea of punk had to do with possibilities—that is, with the question of what was possible at all. Can you say more about that?

Probably like many others back then, I possessed a strong, anti-bourgeois attitude, and when you approach art from that place and have no experience, then the notion of anti-art seems tenable. Or perhaps you long for it without knowing exactly

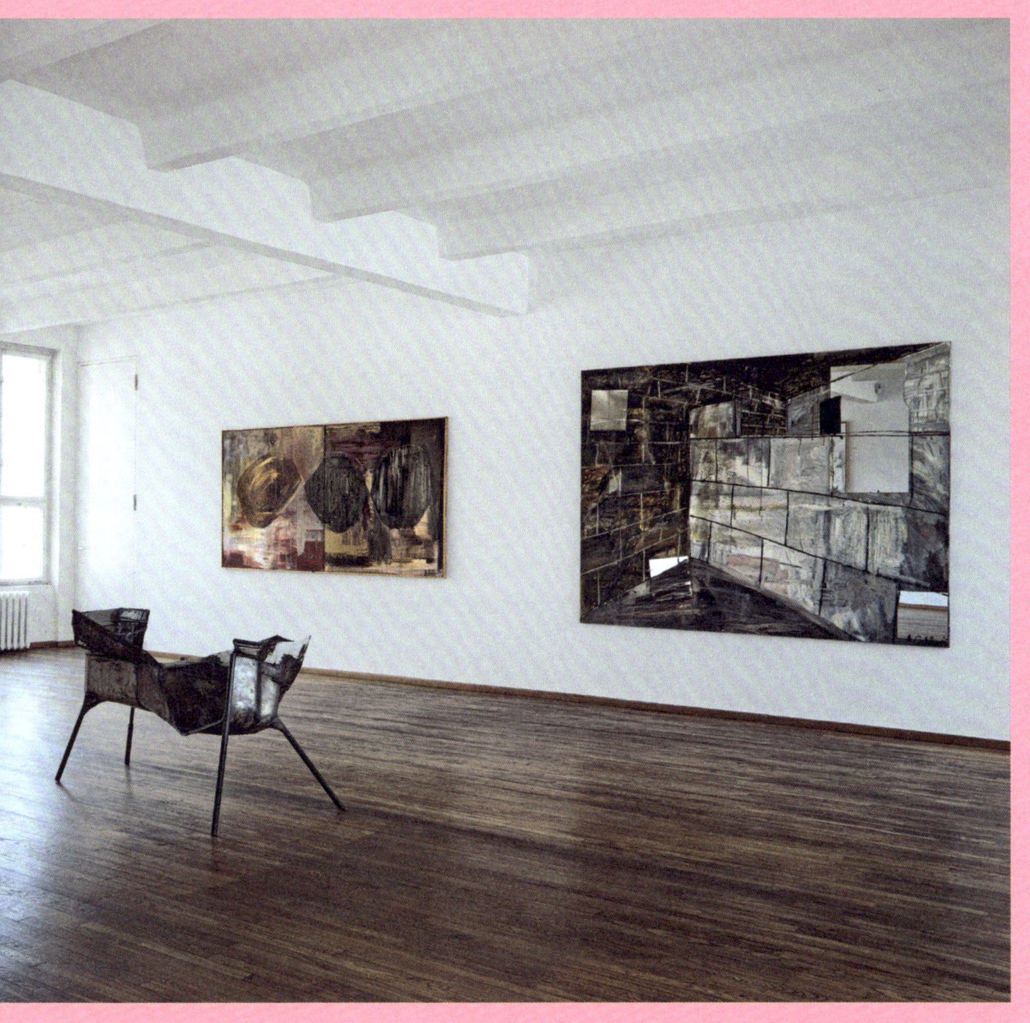

Franz West, *Untitled (Sitz)*, 1988–89
Albert Oehlen, *Auskunft*, 1985
Albert Oehlen, *Untitled*, 1984
Sammlung Hoffmann Installation XX, 2016–17

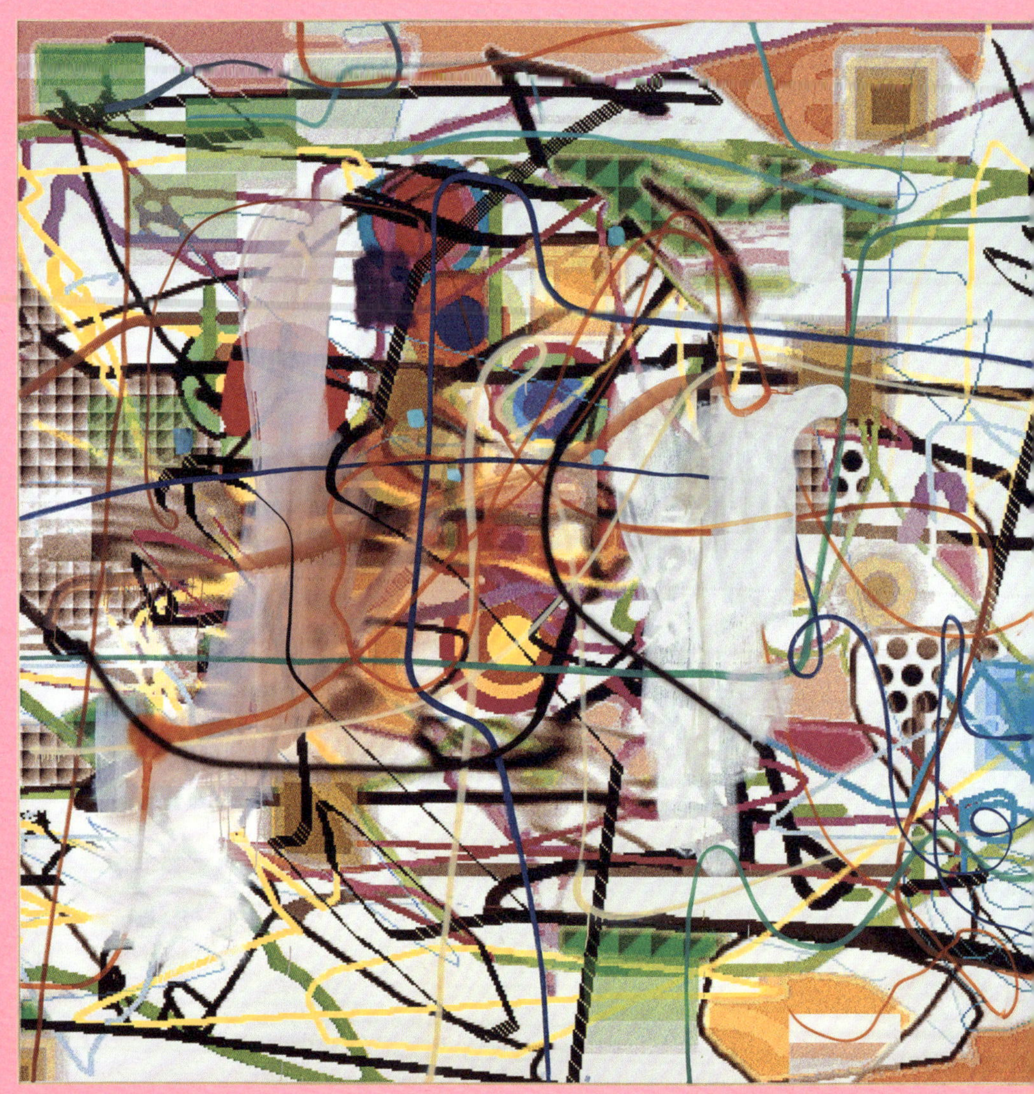

Schwindel, 1996

what it is. If you look at the examples that were around back then, you encounter figures from art history, like Dieter Roth or Joseph Beuys, who were both attacking bourgeois art. At the same time, something was happening in culture that was unpredictable and actually completely independent of whether you listened to punk music or not.

A gesture of protest emerged in a largely unanticipated way, namely through unadulterated stupidity-as-expression. Punks did not argue, they spat. That alone was impossible to deal with! It was simply not foreseeable that a youth culture could exist by reducing itself and its means of expression to an absolute minimum—the absolute, lowest, and stupidest—and all this, quite consciously. That was new.

There's some contradiction in making something consciously stupid.

Because I was also politically engaged as a young person, I was sensitive to forms of resistance. They interested me then, and still do. Funnily enough, left-wing extremism in Germany was a constant battle of demarcation, which meant that excluding one's comrades often became more exciting or important than the actual fight. Observing this made me aware of various forms of expression and how they might apply to art. At some point you realize you have a range of possibilities in front of you: a complete spectrum between aggression and deceit, denial, or whatever.

I'm in no way a punk specialist and it quickly ceased to interest me. Nevertheless, it stimulated my mind. Its total shutdown on and about nothing, of not having to be able to do anything, not having to or wanting to argue anything, reshuffled the cards. That doesn't happen often. A kind of personal renaissance took place.

I would add that at the time there was a lot happening with language in the ways you're describing.

Yes, at the same time, certain terms like "fake" were being discussed. Fake was a byword we were thinking about as we attempted to make anti-art.

When I hear the word fake, I understand it in contrast to authentic or real. Can you explain how it was used back then?

Exactly like that. There were several musical examples of fake at the time. There was *fake jazz* and of course Robert Gordon. *(pauses)* I read something about a method of fighting malaria by catching mosquitoes that carry the disease and, rather than killing them, selecting them from a group and sterilizing the male ones, then sending them off again. I wish that was possible in art!

In the eighties, the term alternative began being used to talk about your paintings. Today, that distinction between mainstream and alternative feels outdated.

I am not so aware of being called alternative. Mainstream, if that's what we call what everyone allegedly loves, is an abomination to me. I'd rather be against that than just alternative.

Does living in the countryside have to do with alternative for you?

No, and when I moved there, I didn't think about my work, I thought about my family. When I went to Spain thirty years ago, I was guided by the impulse that if you can afford it, you should do it. If you can afford an adventure or a change of place—that's some kind of extension of what you know—I just felt, we have to do that. I think that today, too.

One difficult thing about interviews is the expectation that one learns something about the artist. I often feel that when considering your painting and how it's written about, critics attempt to discover something about you as a painter, then interpret that in the work. I have read several texts that focus on who the woman is in *Frau im Baum* (2004).

Absolutely, and that's an issue for me, because such questions don't interest me at all. Each element of a painting like this one has different aspects. You can say that there's a woman's head, but you can also say there are painted newspaper clippings. The tree in the first painting of the series might have had a function, but it could have been something completely different, no? The conventional way to approach a painting is to think that the painting is based on a specific desire to paint something. And that in that desire lies meaning, which is usually assigned to a symbol. If you don't understand the symbol, you think that it's been encrypted and that it has to be cracked, but in my work, this is not the case.

Right, and you are among a number of artists held responsible for explanations, although there might not be any.

Yes, and therein lies the question of whether you need explanations at all.

Painting itself offers unlimited potential for interpretation. I noticed that especially with your Serpentine exhibition [2019–20], I didn't read the exhibition text—couldn't find it, actually—and found it crucial that one couldn't decode things quickly or easily.

Yes, exactly, the exhibition is about that. That is the theme for me. Other artists work with other systems and want different things.

Fantasy is also present in your work, for example, how real topographies are paired and transformed with imaginary ones, or vice versa. I'm thinking of a painting where two different walls intersect [*Untitled*, 1984]. For me, that has as much to do with fantasy as the painting *Schwindel* (1996).

Yes, one imagines fantasy in art as an artist showing something that never been seen. A landscape, for example. But I find that idea quite flat and I'm not sure I have any of that kind of fantasy in me. That imagination for complex, visual things—one either has it, or not, and I don't think I have it.

One finds fantasy in everyday life as well.

Yes, I find fantasy everywhere. I find fantasy when I'm talking to someone, or when I greet someone and try to decipher if they react to me mindlessly or not. You can extend this to anything, and I don't believe fantasy relates only to art. The idea that someone like [Salvador] Dalí and his crazy landscapes might embody the pinnacle of fantasy strikes me as thoroughly naïve.

Can you characterize your teaching style?

I used to hang up pictures with my students in Düsseldorf—that was ten years ago. One student would be asked to hang up a work and we would talk about it together. I asked my students to talk about the work without judging it, in other words, talk as much as possible without saying, "That's crap—or great." The exercise was exhausting for all of us, because sometimes no one wanted to say anything. Overall though we pulled it off and I think it was good. The idea was that a picture could always be meant differently and that something that might have thrown or put one off might have been done purposefully.

This question of what "might be" comes up in your paintings. As a viewer, one has the idea that a painting needs certain things to become a painting—technique or materials, for example. What would you say makes a painting a painting?

That the artist says: "This is a painting."

The video installation *Selbstlos im Lavabad* (Selfless in the Bath of Lava, 1994) got us interested in Pipilotti Rist's work. We saw it at the exhibition *Welt-Moral* in June 1994 at the Kunsthalle Basel: it was there that we suddenly found ourselves standing in front of a small hole in the wooden floor, where, in a split-open plank, a tiny figure of a woman engulfed in flames cried out for help in different languages. As entertaining as some may find the video, I've never been able to laugh about it. Nevertheless, Rolf and I were both enthralled. The images made me think of nineteenth-century illustrations of Dante's *Inferno*.

We acquired the work from Stampa in Basel with a plan to install it in our future Berlin space. Berlin-Mitte, that is, in the former Eastern Sector of the city, where we had bought what had been a factory and wanted to move with our collection. From the beginning, we wanted to live there and share the space with the public. The work came with the artist's condition that she would oversee installation, and that was absolutely fine with us. I arranged to meet Pipilotti in Berlin before we'd actually moved in, in order to determine the placement of the work prior to installing interior walls and wooden floors throughout the space. This was important and practical: we needed to complete the wiring before we laid the flooring and finished the walls. I remember walking through the drafty construction site and, with the help of a blueprint, showing her what we were planning. In the end, we marked a spot that she said would be inconspicuous enough. *Selfless in the Bath of Lava* was supposed to be both surprising and something one might miss. The idea of allowing the public to discover the work on their own without pointing it out fit perfectly with my own view. When visiting our spaces, you really have to put in effort to experience something. It even slightly bothers me when visitors sit on the heaters on the walls, opposite the artwork during tours, seeming to think that art is going to come to them!

During that same visit, I spoke with Pipilotti about a room in which we could present videos that don't require specific installation. My only request was that it not be conceived of as a black box, but instead be infused with light colors. Like the rest of the space, we imagined it as part of a lived-in home, that is, part of our everyday life. She installed a plinth at an angle within the almost-square room, and on top of it she placed a cube made from four huge white canvases on stretcher frames. Seeing moving images projected onto these large canvases really illuminated video's kinship with painting. The thick, white flokati rug Pipilotti selected for the floor invites you to sit and stretch out, then perhaps rest your head on one of five cushions with portraits of our family members—of Rolf, me, and our three children. Pipilotti named it the *Frommer Audiovisionsraum* (Pious Audio Vision Space, 1997), precisely invoking the intimacy that we intended for this room.

As much as Pipilotti's dreamlike installations offer an overwhelmingly seductive aura, luminous color, and surreal storytelling alongside dizzying perspective, her earlier, simpler videos explore inadequacy and a sense of failure that she often heightens in a comedic or grotesque way. In those earlier works, in spite of the magic of her name, of Pipilotti, she loses herself in a frenzy of media: instead of dancing, she falters and falls; instead of singing, she bawls; she writhes from bowel inflammation. These are the works I particularly cherish. *As told to Isabel Parkes*

We all like to bend our memories into particular shapes, but I think I first met Erika and Rolf when they acquired *Selbstlos im Lavabad* (Selfless in the Bath of Lava, 1994), which was an edition of three plus an artist print. At the time, another artist told me that I should make at least ten editions, because the work really finds life when seen in person and one can tower over it and feel like a giant. My experience at Erika and Rolf's loft was good because people could fully experience the work. Their place wasn't completely open to the public, but there were regular group tours. Later, they commissioned me to produce the *Frommer Audiovisual Raum* (Pious Audio Vision Space, 1997). I hope in the meantime they've replaced its technology! Electronic installations are like pets: if the technology is not renewed, the creature dies.

You printed photos of each Hoffmann family member on pillows in that room. Can you say more about changing perspective in order to experience your work? What do you think a change in viewpoint does?

Having an image in front of you is similar to looking out of a window or into your own soul. With the *Pious Audio Vision Space*, I found it exciting that the family could sit on their own heads, so to say, and with that in mind, the question arose as to who's looking at who. That's what interested me. I only really met the whole family once. We shot a video and later the stills became photos, printed on pillows.

Let's talk about *Mutaflor* (1996). The camera's circular motion and the video's looped effect generate both a feeling of spirituality and the chance for a more scientific or mathematical interpretation. What does the circle mean to you?

The circle, or specifically here, the cycle of digestion, symbolizes and reflects how we absorb and process impressions: you keep some with you and let others go. Accepting this letting go means a lot to me. Life follows this process. It comes into being only to quite mercilessly carry on and fade away.

Yes, for me the work touches on consciousness—notions of how external appearances connect with perceptions and feelings which help us understand something bigger.

Exactly, but that's the dilemma! We see a cycle and might be aware of it, but in reality, we are so slow to grasp emotion that we miss the cycle. Only through constant repetition do we understand that everything operates as and in a cycle.

In *Mutaflor*, we don't just understand this idea, but can feel it.

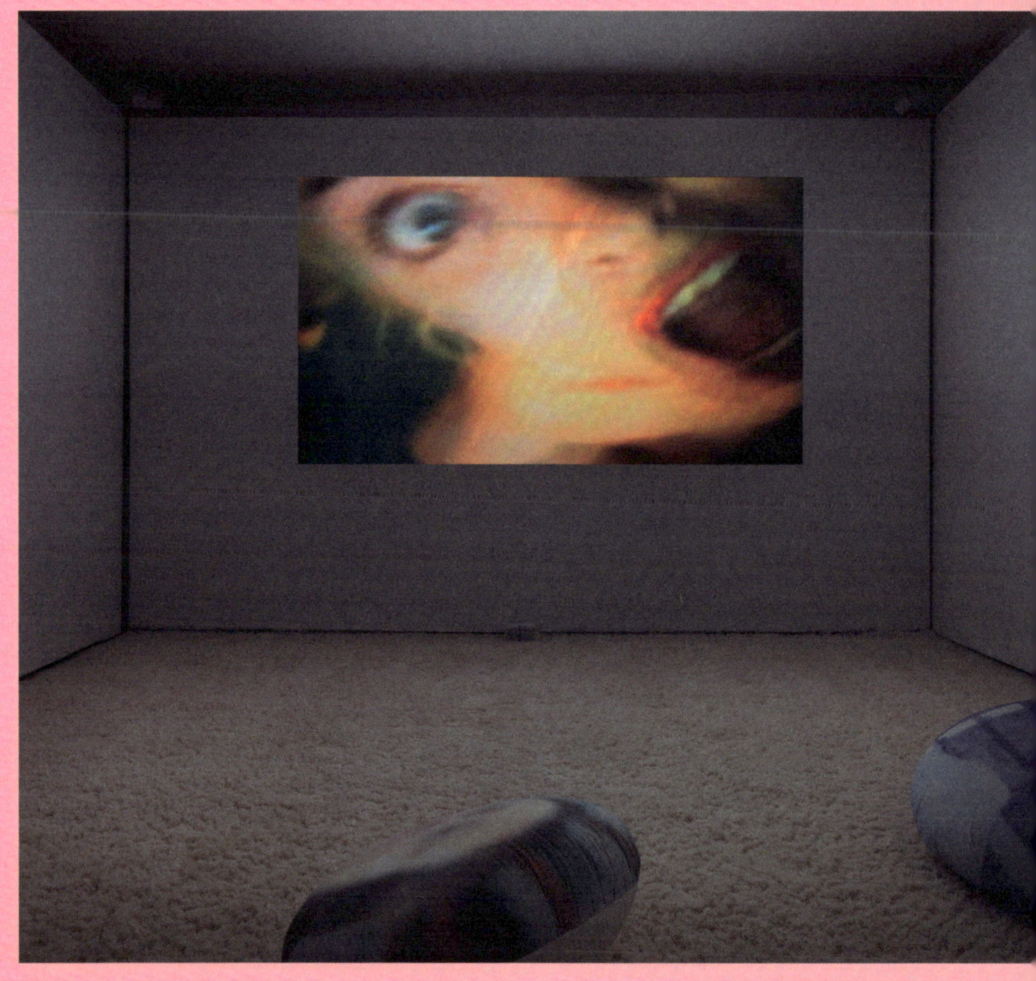

Mutaflor, 1996
installed in *Frommer Audiovisual Raum*
(Pious Audio Vision Space), 1997
Sammlung Hoffmann Installation XII, 2008–09

Yes, both understanding and acceptance are presented vividly in the video through straightforward symbolism and in intentional contrast with more complex, intellectual forms.

What does nudity stand for in your videos?

Nudity reminds us that mankind is a mammal, part of the animal kingdom. Nudity abstracts time and ancestry, with the exception of ethnicity. There is no way to tell what time the person lives in or what social class they come from. Nudity allows us to understand the human being as a philosophical question and points to our very existence. Just think of how often we encounter nudity in early religious paintings or classicism.

Did religion play a role in your upbringing?

Yes, but like many people in the twentieth century, religion was a contradictory part of my life. In school, I had to attend religion classes as well as church, but I remember noticing that my mother didn't herself go. When I was ten or twelve, I became very religious. I went to the Pentecostal Church and read Bible verses and their corresponding interpretations every day. In the evening, I didn't dare fall asleep without having read my Bible beforehand. This was a difficult time for me. I desperately wanted to be a believer, but I constantly had the feeling that I believed too little. I often wished that God would reveal himself to me. Deciding to break away from that all around age thirteen was a huge release. I felt under constant scrutiny, and to a certain extent, I still do. That moment in time left its mark on me.

Can you describe your earliest childhood memory, perhaps the moment you first recall an awareness of self?

I remember two scenes, but am not exactly sure which occurred first. In one, I'm lying in a cot at night in our house on a road in Sedrun, Switzerland. Tanks constantly drove past there because there was a military station nearby and the night I remember, one was particularly loud. I had the feeling that a tank was driving through my room. In the other memory, I take a pitcher and I hit it on the table *(gestures)*. My mother and sister had said something and laughed at me, and I whacked the jug again on the table. It was a red jug with white dots, and it shattered like this *(makes a smashing sound)*. That moment in which my mother and sister suddenly stop laughing is deeply etched in my memory.

Do you remember your dreams?

Yes, I dream a lot and often about some form of religion! In one such dream, I'm in a sprawling city of tents and surrounded by people who I've offended. Those who I've offended very badly are in a red tent, the people who I've offended only slightly are in an orange one, and the others are in a yellow one. I have to go to all the tents and apologize to all the people. That is a dream that has remained especially clear in my memory.

What interests you about fantasy and what form do you think it takes in our world today?

Fantasy is always present and because we can only ever perceive a small portion of reality, we complete the picture with the help of fantasy. For example, if you look at my video *I'm not the Girl Who Misses Much* (1986), you might perceive the image as blurry, but your brain still fills in the gaps. That's how fantasy works here and now. We see each other in high definition. That's what the imagination is for.

Personally, I am most interested in fantasy in terms of asking myself what others see. For example, in the moment when you close your eyes. How can I better understand what others see by looking at works of art? Or vice versa, by looking inward, with my eyes and ears open? This is how I find the material and forms to represent the world around me.

You are yourself the subject of many of your videos, but your work is not really autobiographical. What does it mean conceptually that you cast yourself as one of your work's main characters?

There are several reasons for that, some of which are purely practical. I don't want to have to ask someone to repeat the same thing fifty times! I developed *Selfless in the Bath of Lava* by myself here in the studio. While shooting, I once fell off the ladder and onto my toolbox. I remember thinking, "Yeah, suffer!" Having skin in the game has always been part of it for me.

That sounds like a bit of a punk or a DIY attitude.

Yes, that's true. Very much with the motto that I can do it too or that I can do it alone! I also find a therapeutic quality in that kind of approach and process, which isn't necessarily important for the final product. At the same time, those were moments through which I was able to portray hell with humor, and that offered me an important catharsis.

The character in *Selfless in the Bath of Lava* represents mankind in general, so it is important for me to say that although she is a woman, she also represents man. Normally, women are embodied by women, a reality that relates to societal power

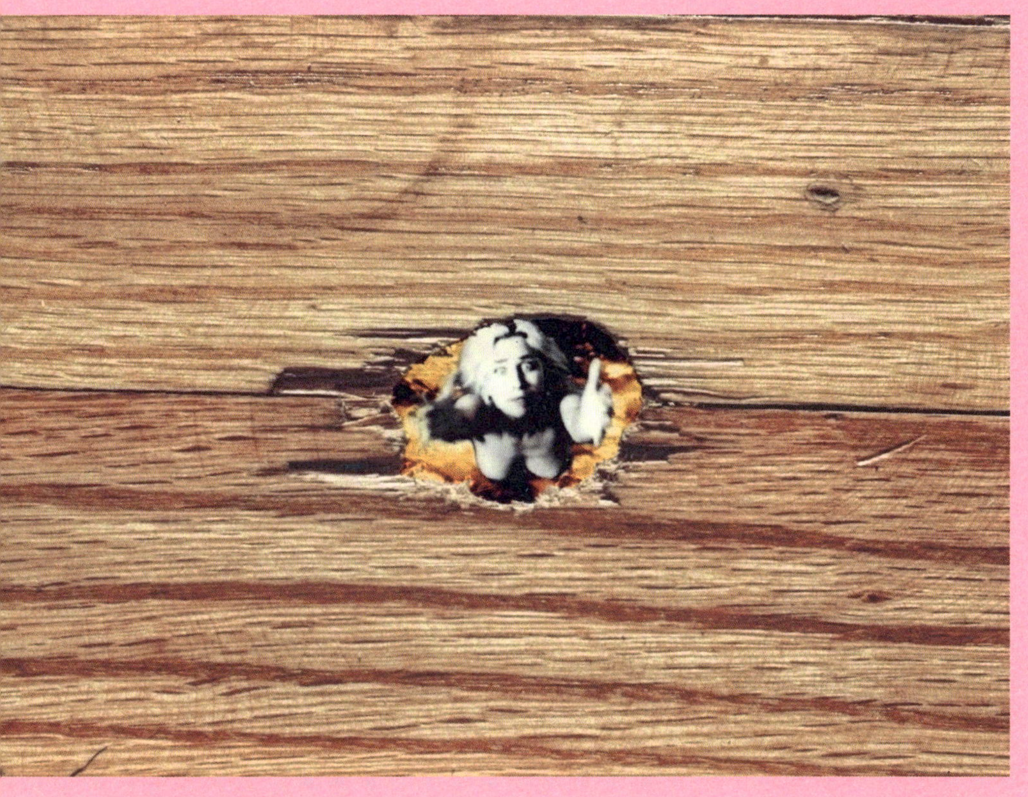

Selbstlos im Lavabad (Selfless in the Bath of Lava), 1994
Sammlung Hoffmann Installation I, 1997–98

structures. It also manifests on a linguistic level. I am called an artist or "Künstler" in German but Gerhard Richter is not called a woman artist or "Künstlerin" in the same language. It will take a few more generations for things like this to change.

Would you say that the change has already begun?

Yes. Billie Eilish is a good example. She doesn't really sell sex but is still mainstream. On top of that, she makes good music. There's definitely something in that combination!

Billie Eilish makes a good bridge for us to talk about questions of participation and sharing online. In what way have technological developments changed your processes?

On a formal level, they have exerted a very strong influence. There was a time in which no one had an LCD monitor, and today, everyone carries one around in their pocket! Knowing that, we presented my work at the New Museum in 2016 on a mobile phone, a little *Bath of Lava*, just like that. Nowadays, many different people can read, see, experience the same story in front of them at the same time. People hardly have to wait for anything anymore. Fashion, for example, is an ever-spinning wheel. Just years ago, it operated with a familiar sequence: first the show, then the outfits hit the stores. But that concept doesn't work anymore. I'm curious to see what really long-term consequences these developments have in terms of content and of course the environment.

What is the importance of physical space for you in this context?

I definitely oppose everything taking place on the Internet, because it really matters to me to enter a space with the body. I am not very present online, because it is too close to my work as a medium. Today, everything is dominated by what I call *speed-ups* and I try the opposite. I work with *speed-downs*. Of course, one can achieve this with technology, but what I mean is that the work should be experienced as light in space. I want the viewer not only to follow the content on a mobile phone screen, but also to perceive the quality of light and become aware of how an image glows out of its plastic. The fact that a projection is just well-organized light, for example, becomes physically comprehensible when you project it onto a body. Personally, I am less concerned with the flipside of content–in other words, its deconstruction. I think it's good that there are artists who are, but I want to use my time to present new possibilities. These include liberating the screen from its most common uses. This rectangle is just a standard that is meant to make us switch between content more quickly. I want to show people that they can be irreverent with technology.

What references are you working with these days?

There is the practical level and the content level. I sometimes visit car showrooms because of their LED displays and the other technical things that hang on their walls. I'm not interested in them in terms of content, but I learn more about professional standards. For me, Es Devlin, the set designer, is an empowering reference. As far as form is concerned, I refer less to the world of contemporary visual arts and more to music and theater. In terms of content, I'm interested in all sorts of fields of knowledge, including statistics and medicine. I am addicted to Wikipedia!

What are you working on at the moment?

Right now, I'm working on two new pieces for MOCA in Los Angeles. One is a floor work and the other is porn! It's kind of a continuation of my *Pickelporno (Pickle Porn,* 1992*),* but infused with my more up to date know-how and old bodies.

What do you consider erotic?

I would really say that *Pickle Porn* (1992) is the only work of mine in which I attempted to generate erotic images. I would more readily use the word sensual for my work. In other words, the pleasure of haptics, of colors, of letting yourself go. Those are all sensual experiences for me, and not necessarily erotic. Eroticism is more about the sexual act. Swimming is something very sensual, so is not being afraid—although one rarely succeeds in that. Laughter is also very important to sensuality.

Can you say more about that? I find that laughing—and playing—are acts that are quickly devalued.

Laughter is closely related to letting go, to an impulsive feeling of complete permeability, which I find very sensual. In fashion photos today, you maybe notice that no one really laughs. Not-laughing is cool. Not-laughing is self-control, is desirable. If a person laughs, he is a desperate salesman. He is not expensive and therefore there is no reason to win him over. These are power games. If one person smiles and the other doesn't, then that person feels they are more powerful. What a joke! You have to put up with the other person taking you less seriously or making you feel like a child—I have often experienced this. And besides, why should we not take children seriously?

FRANK STELLA

It was not until 1977 that Rolf and I saw a work by Frank Stella with our own eyes. It was at Alexander von Berswordt's Galerie m in Bochum and I still remember standing in front of *Leblon II* (1975), which was referred to as a painting but was what I understood as an aluminum relief. I recall how Rolf and I marveled at its bright colors as well as its sliced-up picture plane, in which metal pieces lean against one another at differing angles, so that no piece is ever parallel to the wall; Stella had painted, sprayed, or scribbled on each piece with matte or high-gloss paint. Painting, in other words, was taking place through markedly different techniques, on slanted surfaces which no longer fit in a frame but instead jutted out on all sides. We were really taken by how Stella threw the whole picture into motion. We also detected a social model in it: all kinds of different elements which, although they hardly seemed to correspond with one another, were nevertheless thrust together. Despite Richard Serra's open derision of this so-called "corporate shit," it was for us–and it remains for me–a very important work.

In 1988, once we had stopped working in our company [van Laack], we moved to Cologne, which at the time was a center for contemporary art in Germany. Now, instead of business trips, it was art that made us travel. We not only went to exhibitions, but also looked at many recently built museums in France, Germany, and Switzerland. We were often disappointed by their architecture, mostly because of light. It seemed to us that the old museums were unsurpassable because of their classical architecture, pleasing proportions, particularly of their halls, and soft lighting–think of Kunstmuseum Basel or Kunsthalle Baden-Baden!

We met Frank Stella in person in 1980 at a dinner in Bordeaux, a roaring celebration for the reopening of the city's opera house. There we enjoyed a true feast alongside well-known French winemakers and their very elegant wives and partners, everyone glowing with pride for their magnificent, resurrected opera house. They were highly amused when they learned that we had travelled there to see Stella's exhibition, opening at CAPC [Museum of Contemporary Art of Bordeaux], and to which we had loaned *Leblon II*. Much later, at a smaller dinner in 1991, arranged on the occasion of his exhibition at Hans Strelow's gallery in Düsseldorf, I sat next to Frank. We chatted and I asked him what had been keeping him busy in recent years, he asked what we had been doing, and what some of our ideas for the future were–we simply caught up. After I told him about our plans for a Kunsthalle in Dresden–how we wanted to create an institution for contemporary art, independent from our own collection and whose curators could organize exhibitions with loans from a pool of international collections–I also mentioned that at the time, we were not happy with the proposed architectural designs. Frank simply replied with, "Why can't I do it?" And he immediately started sketching on the paper that covered the table.

It's not that we were particularly convinced that Frank Stella was a good architect. What interested us was to find out what he would want for an exhibition space, what would be important to him as an artist—like with Pipilotti Rist later on with a video room. It seemed like a fantastic opportunity to have someone who dealt with picture planes and space so innovatively be the one to design an exhibition hall. How often had artists complained about the spaces in which they found themselves exhibiting? Saying that nothing was appropriate, or that it was time to tear museums to the ground—that's the kind of thing we heard in the sixties. So, let the artists do it!

As told to Isabel Parkes

How did you meet Erika and Rolf Hoffmann?

How can I answer that? Who can remember? *(pauses)* What brought us together in a serious way was a discussion about the Kunsthalle project in Dresden. That came about in a dinner conversation because Rolf had heard something about me working on a project in the Netherlands for Groningen.

You had already travelled quite frequently to Germany at that time.

Yes, I travelled a lot to Düsseldorf to visit Gabriele Henkel and exhibit with Hans Strelow. Later in the 1970s, I covered a lot of ground as an itinerant F1 fan, and later still came my first museum and gallery shows in Berlin, Munich, and Wolfsburg. You know, I also remember a show in Cologne with Rudolf Zwirner, the highlight of which was Zwirner and Strelow taking us out to dinner and then taking half an hour to decide how to divide the check. Later, Zwirner told someone how impressed he was that I was involved in putting my things on the wall. I've lived too long. Now Zwirner's son has a gallery in New York! *(pauses)* I can't remember, but it must have been that the Hoffmanns went to Dresden to reinforce reunification.

Yes, well Rolf Hoffmann was from Saxony-Anhalt and Erika also has a longstanding interest in early twentieth century Russian art, so Dresden emerged as a choice in terms of geography, history, and culture.

You know, I've been accused of being totally influenced by the Constructivists.

You've been accused of a lot!

Yes, things I said or ignored, like Russian Constructivism! It's an interesting claim because I remember a book by Camilla Gray and a show at the Guggenheim that marked the first mention of the significant impact of Russian art in America. The publication of the book was key because as a text, people as diverse as [Donald] Judd could read it! Outside of the Museum of Modern Art's collection, which was fine but very small and isolated compared to everything else that was going on, the only place you could see Russian work was the Stedelijk Museum in Amsterdam.

But you had already been exposed to artists like Kandinsky.

Yes, through MoMA. I mean how many Constructivist paintings do you have to see to get the idea? It gets interesting after Malevich's *White on White* (1918), but the idea is pretty manifest.

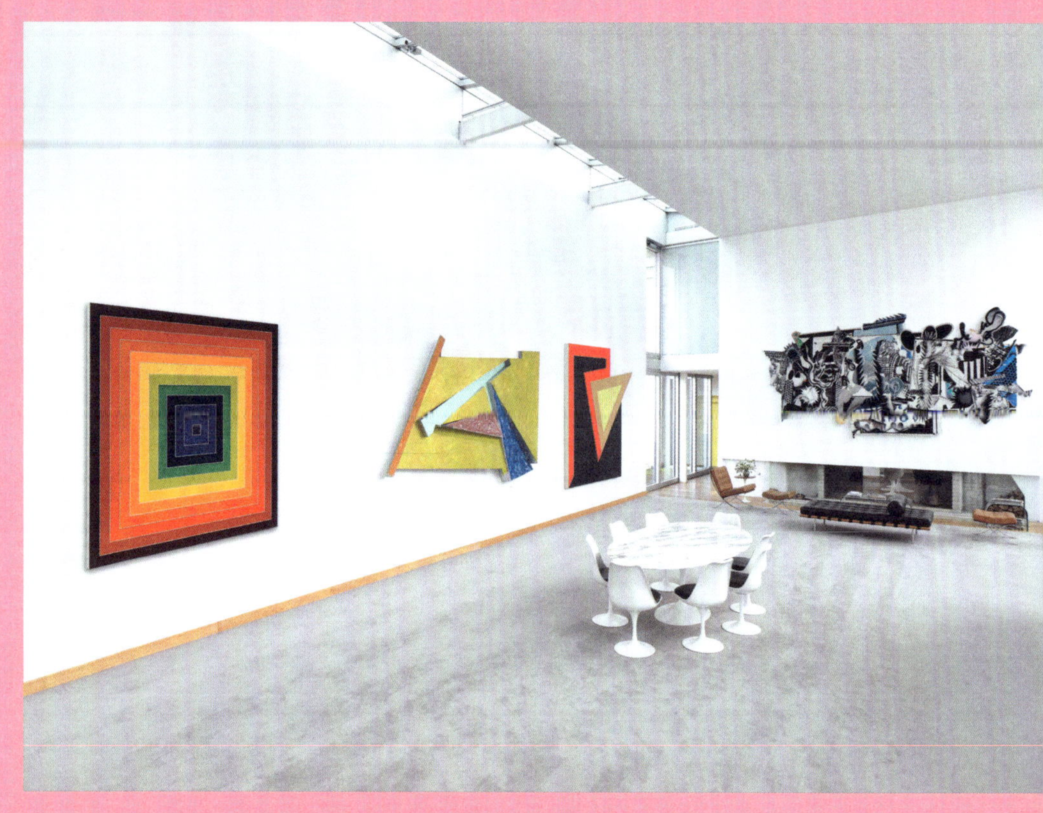

Concentric Squares, 1974
Leblon II (Brazilian), 1975
Tuftonboro I, 1966
The Beggar of Locarno (Nr. 5), Kleist Series, 1999
Sammlung Hoffmann Installation XV, 2011–12

That it's not referring to anything but itself and to making paintings?

Right.

Perhaps also proving that the act of looking translates to the act of painting.

Yes, but that may be true of everything, I don't know. If you're interested in abstraction, then that work gets to the level of the self-evident and that is what abstract art can do. The problem is always that that's what it looks like to somebody who is sympathetic. To someone who's not, it's not doing anything.

But I didn't know the works in the Hoffmann's collection and my involvement was intense with them first in terms of the architecture for the Kunsthalle they were planning to set up in Dresden in the early 1990s. We presented a model and the Dresden people complained that there wasn't an *Allee* and that the paths didn't go straight ahead and that we didn't cut through the garden. That the park had a circuitous path was deemed unacceptable. They wanted it to go through to the Zwinger.

What other feedback did you hear?

A lot of people asked what the rooms would be like if there were going to be curved walls. [Gerhard] Richter thought the colors were outrageous.

Which is funny considering his Cologne windows.

You said it, not me! I think the one who killed it was Kurt Biedenkopf's wife.

What offended her?

She thought it was Disneyworld. It had color and form, two things that were unacceptable. She echoed the sentiment of the planning committee, which was that it didn't have a geometric plan. I got the idea for the forms from [Hermann] Finsterlin and German Expressionist architecture, which one really didn't hear about in Germany at that time.

Was it unusual that you had these references early on?

When I was at school, Bartlett Hayes was the director of Phillip Academy's Addison Gallery, which had an impressive collection that included some advanced examples of twentieth century American art. Hayes was very serious about art education and

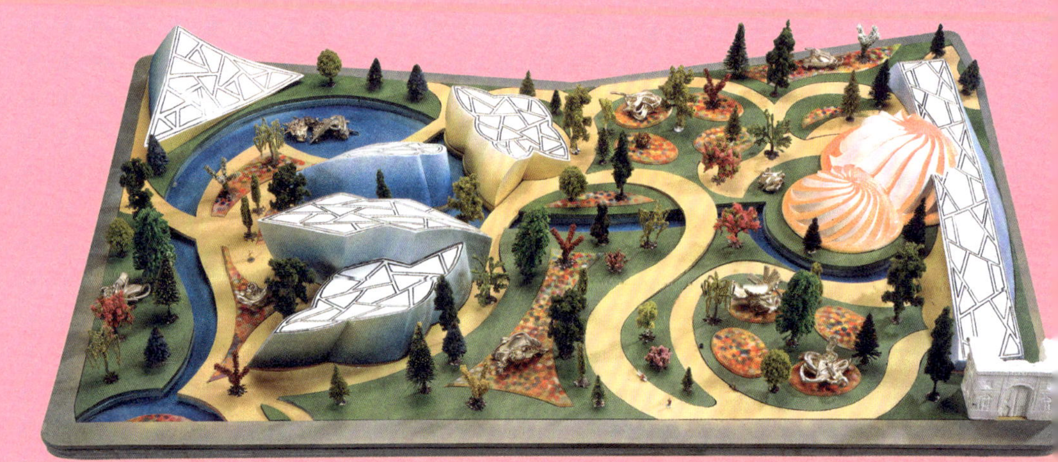

1. Model for Kunsthalle Dresden, 1991

fashioned his department—art history and studio work—along the ideas of Joseph Albers and Hans Hoffmann.

Was this before or after Black Mountain College?

It was probably about the same time. But I never liked Albers.

Why?

I thought it was stupid.

Why?

Well, why wouldn't it be stupid? I mean it was simple division of space with this incredibly ornate color theory that one color influences another. How would one color not influence the color next to it?

So it's too obvious.

Right.

Erika and Rolf collected one of your concentric square paintings, which I find hard to not see in relation to Albers' work.

Yes, that's true, but I leaned toward Hans Hoffmann. His works were tough because they were everything I thought painting should do, but I didn't know how to do it. It took a lot of effort to understand. Well, I got it, but then to know how to make the paint move like that and conceive of color and organization all at the same time was not so easy.

You've had an interesting relationship to paint over the course of your career. What's its starting point?

I used to say, "I'm a painter not an artist," and by painter I meant a house painter. My mother painted, so we did things in oils in the windows and stuff like that, Santa Claus at Christmas or a bunny at Easter. And we made things. My father was a gynecologist but had worked as a house painter through college, so we worked together painting the house and doing repairs. Without knowing it, I was in paint. I never thought much about it. When I went to Andover, I started using paint and smearing it, and that was fine too. It wasn't about being an artist, it was about making something with the material. It wasn't a position or a job, which is a lot different from Germany.

It doesn't seem so interesting now, but it did then, when there weren't so many artists and there was that kind of conflict between representation and abstraction. Making a living as an artist wasn't that easy. Almost everybody had to teach. But if you were a teacher, the ultimate goal was to just be able to paint. To be a teacher was already the goal in Germany. You had a place in society. Being an art teacher in America was nowhere.

You've lived through some significant transformations of the role of the artist.

Yes, it was a lot more *(pauses)* fun and dignified. But you have to have a longer view. It's hard to blame the artist. Blame the culture, blame the people that like that kind of stuff! It's hard for me to understand why they like it, but there are many complicated and not very interesting reasons. Maybe it's the end of elitism or the impact of education on society. Maybe it's the old story of democracy.

The Hoffmanns are in an unusual position in that they would be typical of what used to happen in the United States, which is that collections were amassed with the aim that they would be put together and then destined for public places. But that's gone out of style. People are building their own museums. Which I guess they did in a way. I guess they were right on that trend's line. This further step of the collection going to Dresden will never happen in America. I never thought of that, but it's a big socio-political turning point. It's gone to the state, to the public, fully.

You probably remember that the Hoffmanns open the collection every weekend to tours.

Yes, that was perhaps a little too democratic. But you know, when the art world was smaller, when I was a young artist or something like that, we were invited to the homes and saw the work that people collected. As a young artist in New York, you could go to openings, and then were welcome in the homes of the collectors, where you could get hors d'oeuvres and a drink and see their collection, and then you know, you stopped being invited when you turned thirty somehow, which I think is great. I never really realized it, but it was for the young people and if you hadn't made it by then, you weren't going to Park Avenue for a pig in a blanket.

You've frequently worked in series with an interest in some kind of repetition—

You know, I don't know if it's repetition. It's hard to deny, but I wasn't that interested in that. Blame it all on John Coplans, because if it had only been me no one would have cared, but John made it into a big thing with serial imagery. And that had

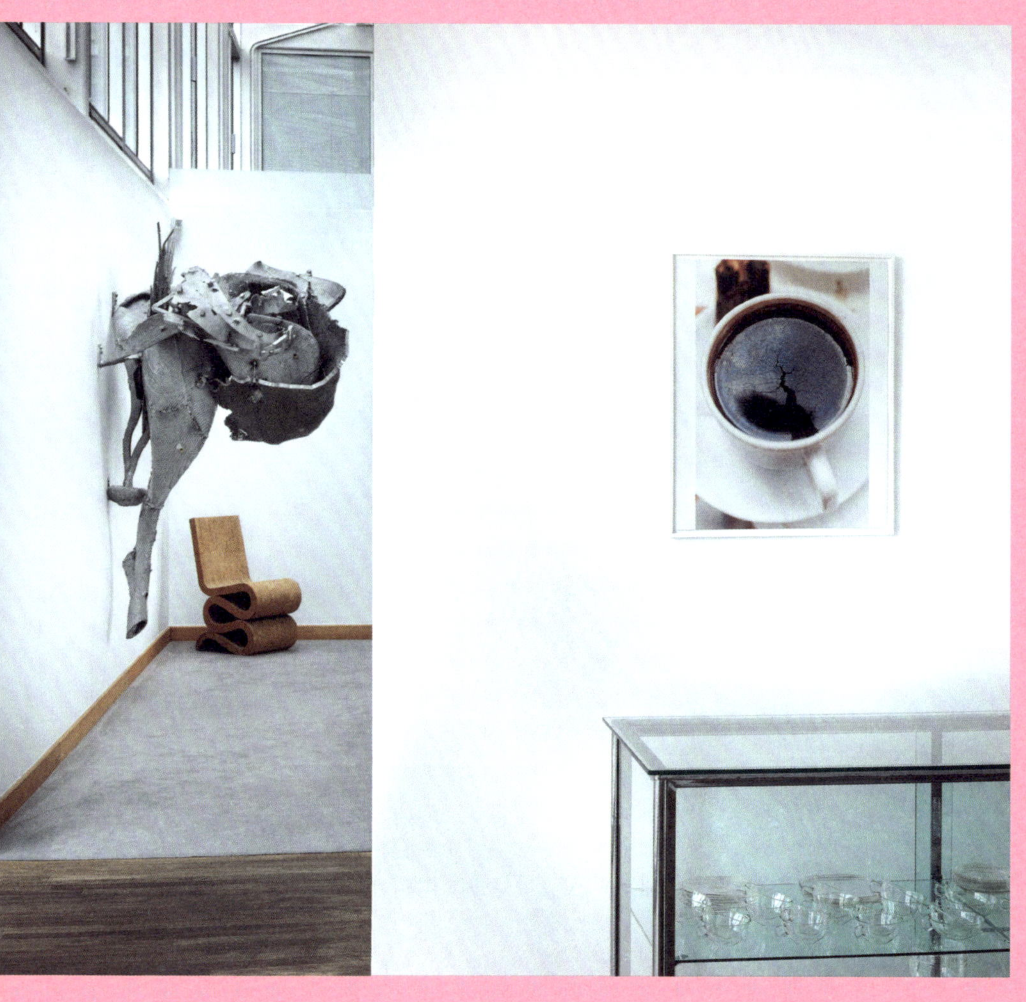

Frank Stella, *"Ei mein Himmel" rief die Alte (Babekan),* Kleist Series, 1998
Frank Gehry, *Wiggle Side Chair*, 1972
Wolfgang Tillmans, *chaos cup*, 1997
Sammlung Hoffmann Installation XVIII, 2014–15

a fair impact and had the advantage of tying the West Coast into the East Coast. It was a big idea.

What has it allowed you to do?

I work and I don't know it's a series. I have an idea and I try a few things. What I often thought were some of the best paintings I ever made were the irregular polygons, and that was a series and then it dropped dead. I couldn't get beyond it.

What is that feeling like?

Once I finished and was thinking, "Well what I do with these ideas or diagrams, where could it go," you know, I made a few drawings, and they just didn't go anywhere. The bottom drops out.

Can you talk about your relationship to pictorial space? You're always solving problems.

That was an interesting part of the sixties: I was an academic painter. Almost all people who were abstract artists were academic. I mean, the accusation was that you were academic. To be a geometric painter—even to be a messy one—was to be academic. And academic was defined then by having an idea and following through, or making the picture be organized. There was a good point there: abstract painting by and large doesn't reveal the process. At the time a lot of great painting was done whereby the process was pretty much the whole thing. I mean, it's not hard to see how a Pollock is done. They don't say very often that the process can be repetitive, but as long as the process was manifest it was good.

And so, removing that process—

Yes, playing it down or not getting into it. The idea was that you were being mechanical. You had an idea and you graphed it out, and then, it was like painting by numbers. You filled in the numbers.

Sounds like an understatement.

Look, it is though. I mean, the problem is to make the numbers interesting. There was also a very strong feeling against having a sense of what you were doing, I guess it's an existential mystique. I loved Friedel Dzubas. We were good friends, and he used to say, "Nah, I'm not going to do that, I just want to get up in the morning and do what I feel like doing." And I said, "So you get up on Monday morning and you do what you feel like, and you get up on Tuesday morning and you do

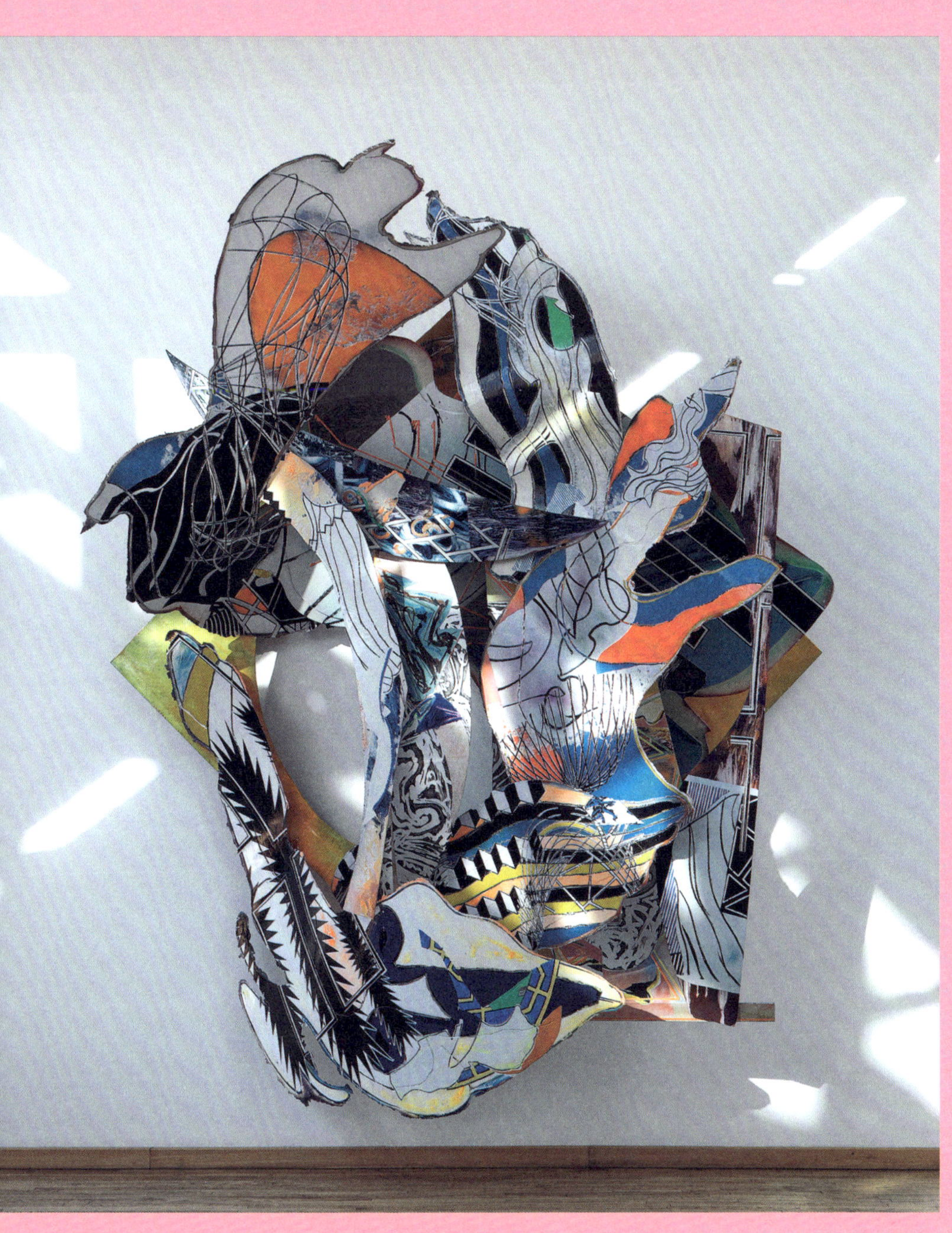

Of Whales in Paint; in Teeth; in Wood; in Sheet Iron; in Stone; in Mountains; in Stars (Moby Dick Series, Chapter 57), 1990
Sammlung Hoffmann Installation I, 1997–98

what you feel like, which is very much like what you did on Monday morning."

How did he respond?

He really laughed.

How did you start your mornings?

Well, I didn't have a problem. If I got up on Monday, I had to paint five stripes over here or whatever it was, and on Tuesday, the other side of the painting.

What marked completion for you, especially in your early days of abstraction?

I had a simple plan. Most of them were symmetrical and I diagrammed them out and I just did them. In the beginning they would change a little bit and after a while they got to be very straightforward and then they got even kind of mechanical for me, so I stopped doing them.

Particularly in the works that Erika and Rolf own, your paintings reveal a strong relationship to other media and disciplines. You've worked with Merce Cunningham, you've made a series inspired by Scarlatti's sonatas. What have those relationships meant to you?

It was a smaller world then and everybody knew everybody. There was a lot going on in the theater and I knew Merce and went to see his dances. And Jasper [Johns] and Bob [Rauschenberg] were involved, too, and Emile de Antonio, a filmmaker, used to produce a lot of the dance things for Merce. You know, it was just part of your social life. Almost every artist that I know from the sixties worked with dancers. And there were of course also the happenings, where artists did their own performances probably based on the theory that, "I can do that better than they can."

What was the draw to Scarlatti?

I got to Scarlatti relatively late and partly because of Ralph Kirkpatrick who organized all the sonatas. I was really attracted to Scarlatti, and I don't even have a great ear, but I liked it and the harpsichord. It's like you can hear every note, or every punch of the fingers. I also liked it because he didn't roll into high gear until he was sixty-five or so. I was sixty-five at the time, thinking of something to do.

How did you discover Heinrich von Kleist?

Kleist was well known and as you remarked, I really went to school. Kleist was great because it was like a movie. Among his famous passages is the opening paragraph, which is a whole page of *The Earthquake in Chile* (1807). It's an endless sentence and Kleist's stories played into the idea of the shapes. It must have been around the same time that I was working on *Moby Dick*, thinking that shapes could act on their own level or present themselves as an event or story. That was giving shape character. That lessened the burden of abstraction, of being unidentifiable.

There's a slow move towards not the literal but the descriptive.

I think so. But that's also a way of giving a painting its own kind of life.

When you describe shapes as events, I'm thinking about *Of Whales in Paint and Teeth* (1990), installed in Erika and Rolf's living room.

It just seems that the piece works in that it has a little bit of what it's like to be at sea or on the ocean. It changes the scale and the relationships of objects to each other and to you. They seem larger than they actually are, those works. When they come together, they start to loom over you. There's a feeling that you're moving into active space.

And there's a liquidity in the sculpture, which in some ways refers to the process of applying paint.

Yes *(looking around his studio at recent work).* These are a little less painterly, I suppose, but I can't paint like I used to, the physicality is not there.

What is the relation of this new work to your past experiences with paint?

It's another kind of geometry. That *(pointing to a large sculpture)* is from smoke, from smoke rings. Smoke is a version of a wave. It's all about motion and turbulence and those kinds of things, because you want painting to have a sense of vitality and movement. That's what everybody wants.

Do you mean that's what you want as a painter?

When people say they want feeling in a painting that's what they mean. That there's something they can relate to. Now it's gone over the top.

You've worked continuously through periods of immense technological change.

I suppose it's true, but I don't get very far on my phone.

I don't mean your phone.

I have two people who help me and we use a lot of 3D printing. Today it's easy to make complicated models.

What's the problem you're solving these days in your work?

There's no problem in the work. The problem is in the overall thing in which—it's hard to say—in which there's a level at which I think it's okay, but I don't quite get the kick of the satisfaction that I used to get in the old days. I don't know if that has to be with being old. It seems okay to me, but when something used to work out and was good that was kind of exciting. I don't know how to put it, it's maybe not fair. I don't think the excitement is gone because the work is not good enough. It probably is, or maybe it isn't, I don't know. It's just not quite as satisfying making things.

Can you imagine going back to two dimensions?

A lot of other people can, my wife among them. Everyone says why don't you paint on a flat canvas. I get a lot encouragement in that direction.

What's stopping you?

I don't know how to do it! I couldn't even imagine where to begin.

WOLFGANG TILLMANS

As intriguing as I find Wolfgang Tillmans's photographic wall installations with their fluid combination of varied sizes, motifs, and media, I always try to look at his photographs individually. In the beginning, when he was photographing for *i-D Magazine* and others, I was especially captivated by his pictures of people his own age—of couples and groups—because I had the impression that he not only observed his generation closely but, by depicting his peers, also exerted an influence on how they represented themselves.

In the early nineties, Rolf wasn't yet convinced by Tillmans's work, just as, incidentally, he wasn't convinced by Rineke Dijkstra's, which he considered to be nothing more than snapshots or documentary photographs and therefore not art! This was not an uncommon opinion at the time, just as much as today, it goes without saying that these are works of art. Tillmans, in any case, really mastered the aesthetics of snapshots, but created a very direct, unaffected impression without allowing his photographs to be "mere" snapshots. In spite of his skepticism, Rolf was not opposed to acquiring the odd work, especially because they were affordable. With these, I was soon able to convince him not only of the contemporaneity of the subjects but also of their autonomy, of the work's sheer necessity, and Wolfgang's mastery of the medium—criteria which we usually discussed before any acquisition. Apart from the gifts we gave each other, which were meant to be surprises, we bought nothing that we hadn't come to an agreement about, even if this involved debates that stretched over weeks.

Today, some of these pictures are considered icons of the 1990s, images that have shaped our perception of youth culture of the time. The photographs of Tillmans's friends, their games and parties, street and beach scenes, interiors, and the 303 Synthesizer each tell me about experiences that I did not have but which were characteristic for his generation and thus for our childrens'. I received my first photograph by Wolfgang Tillmans, *Knotenmutter* (Knot Mother, 1994)—which was taken right in our neighborhood in Cologne—as a gift from our daughter Corinna. What Tillmans meant by it was clear to her, because his photographs captured qualities essential to her experience, and I found her assessment thoroughly convincing.

After this, I followed what Tillmans seized on. He never gets stuck on a subject or a technique, but always tries new things. This is something that I also value, for example, with Isa Genzken and Frank Stella: they keep moving, they constantly expand their potential. I was particularly delighted by Wolfgang's abstract images, *Blushes*, which one can barely call photographs. Rather, they involve more or less accidental traces of dust and light. I am impressed by this radicality.

How do you look at the world? Tillmans is there where something is happening that seems important to him, and he is able to keep an eye on everything at once. *As told to Isabel Parkes*

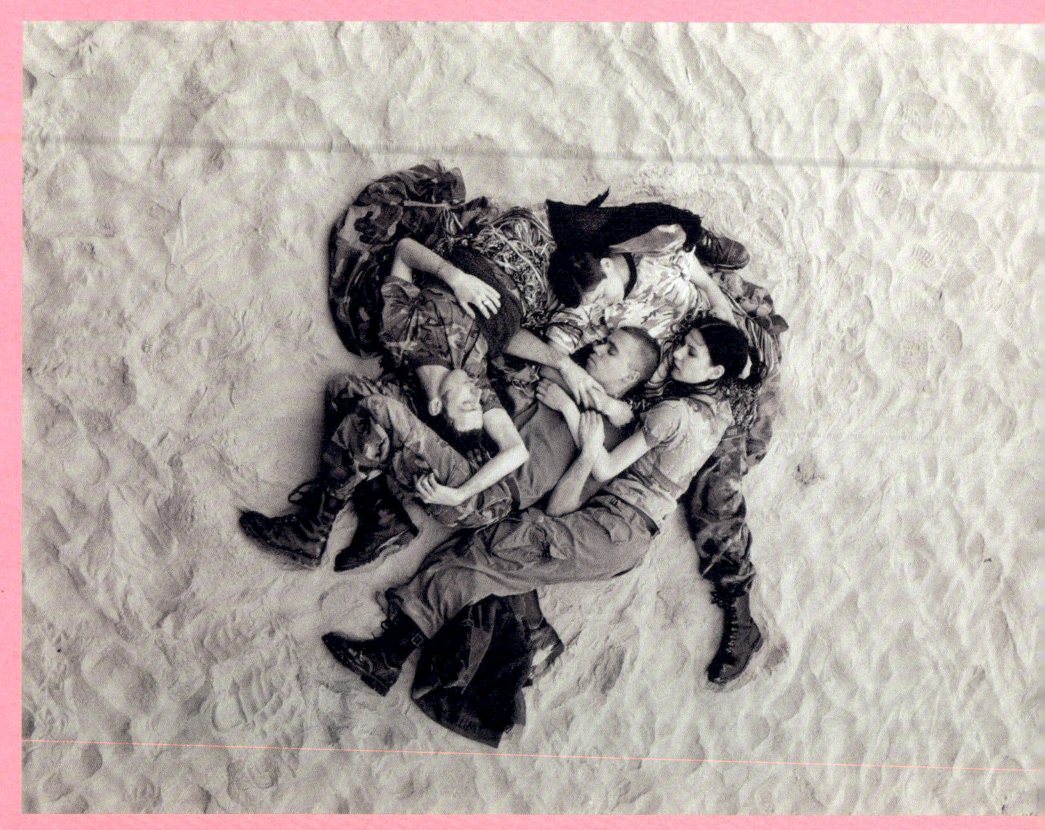

Lutz, Alex, Suzanne & Christoph on beach (b/w), 1993

I think their daughter Corinna was the first to buy my work, but I met Erika and Rolf Hoffmann in 1993 during the November art fair in Cologne. They hosted a reception in their home, and I remember being introduced to Astrid Klein and asking, "*the* Astrid Klein?" and Erika replied, "Yes." It wasn't that Astrid was incredibly famous, but for me as a young artist who had seen her work for years in Hamburg's subway station, it felt exciting. That was the first full year that I was part of the Cologne art world, showing with Daniel Buchholz. The area in which they lived, Belgisches Viertel, was nearby to Daniel's place, and in those days, I crashed on his floor. Isa Genzken and Gerhard Richter lived 300 meters down the road and Hallmackenreuther, the bar where everybody went, was just on Brüsseler Platz.

What I liked about Erika and Rolf, and later Erika, was how they followed my work and kept track of its changes. In 2001 I had an exhibition at Andrea's [Andrea Rosen Gallery] in New York, in which I showed predominantly non-figurative, non-camera-based works. They bought two or three. It was encouraging to see people getting these minimal *Blush* pieces because at that time it wasn't clear that they would become a group of works that would carry on for the next twenty years. Erika and Rolf have always been open and adventurous collectors. I think the variety of subject matter and different formats I use require that collectors engage with all that is going on and make informed choices about my work, rather than just look for signature pieces.

What has that kind of support from collectors offered you as an artist, beyond the obvious?

Fundamentally the act of buying art is transactional and we—me, Daniel [Buchholz], Andrea [Rosen], Maureen [Paley]—always believed in what I exhibited. While I've always been grateful for purchases, which in turn finance the viability of my projects, I don't know if I would call it "support." Support makes me think of fans, of teams. They put their money behind an artist like a fan puts an annual ticket behind a team. All the artists in a collection collectively make the status of the collection itself. The Hoffmanns saying, "We want this twenty-five-year-old in our collection" gave me a sense of confidence.

Today you are known for supporting younger artists by buying their work as well as offering them platforms.

I have always loved art. The reason that I want to be in it and why I make work is to contribute to art—not only to see myself on the wall, but to see myself in the context of what has been and what will be on the wall. I've learned from collectors who collect my work that the arts need money to be made, to exist. So, from a certain point on, around 2000, I felt it was important to somehow be part of that process: buy work or donate, make an edition, open Between Bridges (in 2006), and teach at Städelschule.

I feel it is vital to be involved in art beyond just making or producing. When you see it multilaterally, it's obvious that you can't think of collectors as the so-called other side. Good collectors play a vital role in what goes on and are respected not just because they buy art, but for their taste and spirit and intellect. There are also collectors who open spaces and institutions, which shifts the balance. These collectors take on a different or expanded role which sometimes can interfere with cultural structures and institutions, for example in Germany, between a Kunstverein, Kunsthalle, and Kunstmuseum.

It seems relevant to say that Erika and Rolf's collection will be donated to the State Museums of Dresden.

Yes, and that gets at what I wanted to say: the Hoffmanns remained these interested and interesting—and resolutely private—people, to this date in Erika's case. They haven't become, in my eyes, operators who suddenly place additional pressure on artists to deal with what they want to do with their collection. I don't mean to talk down what other private collections or foundations do, but it can create work. Over the past ten or so years, these kinds of collectors' spaces have changed the flow of traffic and determined shows in a way that previously, public institutions did.

On the other hand, private museums have existed all along. In terms of the Sammlung Hoffmann, theirs was always clearly a private, lived-in home. I liked that I never knew if my work was hanging or not. There was simply not a fuss made, and they were very respectful about actually not involving me as an artist. *(pauses)* Sometimes, there can be a sense that when you buy a work from an artist, you also buy a piece of that artist, and that you can always somehow access them.

It strikes me that particularly in the photographs in the Sammlung Hoffmann, you've long emphasized groups of people and moments of collaboration. The relationship between your subjects and how you live your life feels close.

A sense of togetherness was and is a major interest of mine. In other words, how people interact together, how they can have fun together, how they can have fun for free without buying into or consuming anything. I'm interested in how people can achieve things working together. *Sitzkreis*, for example, is a game that tests if everybody playing can sit in a group while sitting on each other's knees and forming a circle. *operation*

Blushes #5, 2000

theater I, which depicts open-heart surgery, also interested me in terms of a group of people, although in a very different way.

Can you tell me more about deciding when and how to frame your photos?

Until 1999, I relied on three distinct ways to hold a sheet of paper on the wall without framing: C-prints were taped, photocopies and magazine pages held with steel needles, and the large, unframed inkjet prints held with binder clips. I was driven to do so by my love for the sheet of paper as an object, as sculptural matter, and as a skin. I wanted to celebrate the fragility and the beauty of paper, which for me has to do with a certain minimalism rather than grunge aesthetic. This purity of the unframed object can only be maintained for a few months. After that, its surface, which is made of gelatin in the case of C-type prints, wants to absorb the humidity and whatever comes with it. It attracts pollution, for example.

It's entropic.

Exactly, and more alive than one wants it to be. Putting a print in a frame is actually closer to my intention than leaving it unprotected over time. That seems contradictory, but the temporal aspect changes things. I guess it relates closely to how I look at most everything in my work and in my life: we strive for clean answers, black and white, yes or no, but in reality, when you factor in different parameters, we find that things aren't so easily divisible.

This notion might relate to how you have used *Untitled* both in and as a title for your work.

It could. On one hand, I pursued titles matter-of-factly early on. I liked the poetry of just saying what an image is in as few words as possible and not offering a direct interpretation. For example, not *Lutz, Alex, Suzanne & Christoph* "cuddling" or "romantic" *on beach*, just "on beach." I write most titles in lowercase, which, in the English language, is downright incorrect. This often means my work gets accessioned incorrectly, but I like the elevation that a title gives something. The act of titling can become anti-formal in a way that becomes its own formalism.

I was familiar with concepts of titling early on and was always interested in what Felix Gonzalez-Torres or Carl Andre were doing. It is something I think many artists look to other artists for: how artists make something their own. It's also of course part of the enigma of certain artists.

The few times I chose *o.T.* [ohne Titel] or *Untitled* were not in direct reference to anyone or anything in particular, although in the two cases of the works Erika owns, they were both very close to Jochen Klein's death. Maybe they were charged with something or maybe I didn't want to give any charge. I also made "Untitled" works later, so I don't want to say that something untitled only equates to a particularly devastating time. I would sooner say it was a strategy to highlight something one chooses not to do or what one does do—that one is free to play with choice. In fact, very close to the time that I made *o.T. München* and *untitled (La Gomera)*, I made *chaos cup*, which is an example of a deliberately poetic title (all 1997).

Can you talk about your editing process?

There isn't one but in general I think the main thing for me is to have checks and balances at hand, operating in my mind's background in order to help separate wishful thinking from reality. Reality is the wrong word in terms of choosing an artwork, but maybe wanting, a greedy wanting for a picture to be good. We are continually hoping that what we do today is as good as the great thing we did five years ago. That is the ultimate challenge and motivation. It's the spring that never loses tension and that moves us to carry on. That is the hope. When you look for success, it might blind you to the less-loud, less-direct, or obvious work. So, I also try to mistrust my criteria and my desires when editing.

This combination of hope and desire seems to hinge on optimism.

I think hope and desire are integral to the work and to the process of creating, and what we call optimism. Nonetheless, I don't feel a restless desire at the core of my work. I feel it's more about stillness and attention. It is not about trying to control a certain perspective about the world through pictures, it's more that I'm trying to bear the multiplicity of things and let them stand on their own. In that way, it's more about giving up control, being witness to the fact that there are no simple answers and celebrating that complexity. So, I'm an optimist and I think my work is optimistic, but in a fragile sense.

Your mention of mistrusting desires also makes me think about how you use Instagram, which is different from many other artists.

In most cases, these pictures are not really my work in that they don't appear in books or exhibitions. Still, I notice that people take them much more seriously than I do. The platform allows me to be an amateur photographer. It allows me to put out a perhaps careless or playful picture. Initially, I thought I would only include pictures of text on Instagram and then

Silver 105, 2012

my first image ended up being a snowman melting. I found it refreshing. Now it has become a language of its own.

The combination of sharing something playful and urgent reiterates what you were saying earlier about how apparent contradictions coexist.

Yes, an image can be both playful and a campaign medium. Recently I haven't posted much on the platform. However potent it can be, it's okay not to use communication channels at all times.

The SAMMLUNG HOFFMANN is an art collection based in Berlin since 1997, when Erika and Rolf Hoffmann moved into and began opening their home to the public. Although collecting art was not their intent when they made their first purchases in the late sixties, the couple's shared interest in art's capacity to both reflect and inform society, and their longstanding relationships with artists have shaped what is today one of Germany's most significant holdings of contemporary art. In the wake of her husband's death in 2001, Erika Hoffmann-Koenige continued what the couple started together. In 2018, she announced the decision to donate some 1,200 pieces of the collection to the State Museums of Dresden.

ISABEL PARKES is a British-American curator, producer, and writer who worked with the Sammlung Hoffmann between 2012 and 2015 as an educator and editor. Other institutional affiliations have included Performance Space New York, Creative Time, Lincoln Center for the Performing Arts, and Uferhallen-Berlin. Isabel writes for *Artforum* and *Frieze*, among other publications. This is her second book of interviews.

Monica Bonvicini, *Leather Hammer #1*, 2004
Hammer wrapped in leather, 30×10 cm
Photo: Thomas Seidel; Courtesy Schenkung Sammlung Hoffmann, Staatliche Kunstsammlungen Dresden
© Monica Bonvicini and VG Bild-Kunst, Bonn

Monica Bonvicini, *NOT FOR YOU*, 2006
Galvanized steel, light bulbs, dimmer, electrical cables, 300×74.3 cm; *Pavillon*, 2002, steel construction, black leather, chains
Photo: studioschuurman; Courtesy Sammlung Hoffmann, Berlin
© Monica Bonvicini and VG Bild-Kunst, Bonn

Katharina Grosse, *Sie trocknen ihre Knie mit einem Kissen* (They dry their knees with a pillow), 2012
Acrylic on wall, 600×1600×850 cm
Untitled, 2011, acrylic on canvas, 240×388 cm
Photo: Jens Ziehe; Courtesy Sammlung Hoffmann, Berlin
© Katharina Grosse and VG Bild-Kunst, Bonn

Katharina Grosse, *Untitled*, 2006
Acrylic on acrylic resin and styrofoam, 103.5×92×163 cm
Schenkung Sammlung Hoffmann, Staatliche Kunstsammlungen Dresden
© Katharina Grosse and VG Bild-Kunst, Bonn

Roni Horn, *From Some Thames*, 2000 (detail)
Photograph on paper, UV-lacquer; 4 images, each: 63.5×96.5 cm
Photo: unknown; Schenkung Sammlung Hoffmann, Staatliche Kunstsammlungen Dresden

Roni Horn, *Paired Gold Mats – For Ross and Felix*, 1995
99.99 fine gold foil, 2 units, each: 49×60×0.00098 in
Photo: unknown; Schenkung Sammlung Hoffmann, Staatliche Kunstsammlungen Dresden

Roni Horn, *Deeps and Skies*, 1995–96
Solid optical glass, 20.3×76.2×101.6 cm; *Blake's Burn*, 1994–95, solid 6061 aluminum and solid epoxy plastic, 2 elements, each: 11.4×66×91.4 cm; *Untitled #3*, 1998, iris printed photograph, 2 parts, each: 56×56 cm; *Untitled #1 (Ravens)*, 1998, iris printed photograph, 2 parts, each: 56×56 cm; *From Some Thames*, 2000, photograph printed on paper, UV lacquer, 4 images (each) 63.5×96.5 cm
Photo: Jens Ziehe; Courtesy Sammlung Hoffmann, Berlin

Roni Horn, *Blake's Burn*, 1994–95, solid 6061 aluminum and solid epoxy plastic, 2 elements, each: 11.4×66×91.4 cm
Photo: unknown; Courtesy Sammlung Hoffmann, Berlin

Katarzyna Kozyra, *Olympia*, 1996
(3 panels) Light jet laser print on Endura paper on alu-sheet on wood, framed, each: 180×240 cm
Video with sound, 7:27 min
Photo: Artist; Schenkung Sammlung Hoffmann, Staatliche Kunstsammlungen Dresden

Katarzyna Kozyra, *The Rite of Spring*, 1999
6-channel video installation, sound, 32 sec. loop
Photo: Jens Ziehe; Sammlung Hoffmann, Berlin

Katarzyna Kozyra, *Looking for Jesus*, 2013–
Video, 68:33 min
Photo: Artist; Schenkung Sammlung Hoffmann, Staatliche Kunstsammlungen Dresden

Julie Mehretu, *Manifestation*, 2003
Ink and acrylic on canvas, 183.5 × 244.5 × 4 cm
Photo: Jens Ziehe; Sammlung Hoffmann, Berlin

El Lissitzky, *Proun*, ca. 1920
Gouache and mixed media on cardboard, 70 × 43.5 cm
Schenkung Sammlung Hoffmann, Staatliche Kunstsammlungen Dresden

Ernesto Neto, *Nave Óvulo Organóide*, 1998
Lycra tulle, cotton rope, hooks and buttons, ground pepper, and clove, Styrofoam, approx. 340 × 450 cm
Courtesy Sammlung Hoffmann, Berlin

Ernesto Neto, *paff puff and the eternal infinite*, 1998
Lycra and spices, dimensions variable; *Untitled (Dry Color Field)*, 2005, cotton and plastic strings, 220 × 395 cm; *Follicle Ovaloid (Pete)*, 1998, stocking and Styrofoam, 231.1 cm high, diam. 121.9 cm; *Follicle Ovaloid (Lili)*, 1998, stocking and Styrofoam, 246.4 cm high, diam. 101.6 cm
Photo: Jens Ziehe; Courtesy Sammlung Hoffmann, Berlin

Ernesto Neto, *Colônia*, 1988
Lead pellets in nylon stockings, dimensions variable; Matthew Ritchie, *A Glorious Martyrdom Awaits Us All at the Hands of Our Tender and Merciful God*, 2003, oil and marker on canvas, 223.5 × 251.5 cm; Gotthard Graubner, *Brazen Snake*, 1985 Voluminous color form: acrylic, oil and ink on canvas on synthetic cotton wool, 255 × 255 × 12 cm
Photo: Jens Ziehe; Courtesy Sammlung Hoffmann, Berlin

Mike Kelley, *Figure/Ground*, 1990, two parts: mixed media, 183 × 180 × 23 cm, 183 × 160 × 25 cm; Albert Oehlen, *FN 29*, 1990, oil on canvas, 214 × 214 cm; *FN Romantic*, 1990, oil on canvas, 214 × 214 cm
Photo: Jens Ziehe; Courtesy Sammlung Hoffmann, Berlin

Franz West, *Untitled (Sitz)*, 1988–89; Albert Oehlen, *Auskunft (Information)*, 1985, oil on canvas, 130 × 260 cm; Albert Oehlen, *Untitled*, 1984, oil-enamel paint and mirror on canvas, 188 × 260 cm
Photo: studioschuurman; Courtesy Sammlung Hoffmann, Berlin

Albert Oehlen, *Schwindel*, 1996
Inkjet print and oil on canvas, 243 × 241 cm
Schenkung Sammlung Hoffmann, Staatliche Kunstsammlungen Dresden

Pipilotti Rist, *Mutaflor*, 1996
Video, ca. 2 min loop; as seen in: Pipilotti Rist, *Frommer Audiovison Raum*, 1996, mixed media, approx. 300 × 500 × 490 cm, 5 pillows: 70 × 36 cm
Photo: Jens Ziehe; Courtesy Sammlung Hoffmann, Berlin

Pipilotti Rist, *Selbstlos im Lavabad* (Selfless in the Bath of Lava), 1994
Video installation, sound, 12 × 11 × 7 cm, duration 1:08 min as loop
Courtesy Sammlung Hoffmann, Berlin

Frank Stella, *Concentric Squares*, 1974
Acrylic on canvas, 7.8 × 204.7 × 204.4 cm; *Leblon II (Brazilian)*, 1975, lacquer and oil on aluminum, 20 × 210 × 340 cm; *Tuftonboro I*, 1966, synthetic polymer paint and graphite on canvas, 255 × 277 × 10 cm; *The Beggar of Locarno (Nr. 5), Kleist Series*, 1999, collage on paper on wooden structure, 240 × 508 cm
Photo: Jens Ziehe, Courtesy Sammlung Hoffmann, Berlin
© Frank Stella and VG Bild-Kunst, Bonn

Frank, Stella, *1. Model for Kunsthalle Dresden*, 1991
Mixed media on wooden board, 15 × 123 × 86 cm
Schenkung Sammlung Hoffmann, Staatliche Kunstsammlungen Dresden
© Frank Stella and VG Bild-Kunst, Bonn

Frank Stella, *"Ei mein Himmel" rief die Alte (Babekan),* Kleist Series, 1998, honeycomb and cast aluminum, 132 × 213.4 × 152.4 cm; Wolfgang Tillmans, *chaos cup*, 1997, C-print, 65 × 54 cm
Photo: Jens Ziehe, Courtesy Sammlung Hoffmann, Berlin
© Frank Stella and VG Bild-Kunst, Bonn

Frank Stella, *Of Whales in Paint; in Teeth; in Wood; in Sheet Iron; in Stone; in Mountains; in Stars* (Moby Dick Series chap. 57), 1990, mixed media on aluminum
439 × 345 × 201 cm
Photo: Jens Ziehe, Courtesy Sammlung Hoffmann, Berlin

Wolfgang Tillmans, *Lutz, Alex, Suzanne & Christoph on beach (b/w)*, 1993
Chromogenic print, 30.5 × 40.6 cm

Wolfgang Tillmans, *Blushes #5*, 2000
Chromogenic print, 61 × 50.8 cm

Wolfgang Tillmans, *Silver 105*, 2012
Chromogenic print mounted on Dibond aluminum in artist's frame, 181 × 236 × 6 cm
Courtesy Sammlung Hoffmann, Berlin

Back cover: Gunda Förster, *5 Passageways* (Light spaces in the Sophie-Gips-Höfe's passageways), 1996–97, yellow, red, blue neon lights
Courtesy Sammlung Hoffmann, Berlin

So let the artists do it.
Conversations with ten artists from the Sammlung Hoffmann and Erika Hoffmann-Koenige, the collector who let them

Editor
Isabel Parkes

Design
Hanzer Liccini

Texts
Erika Hoffmann-Koenige,
Isabel Parkes, conversations with Monica Bonvicini, Katharina Grosse, Roni Horn, Katarzyna Kozyra, Julie Mehretu, Ernesto Neto, Albert Oehlen, Pipilotti Rist, Frank Stella, Wolfgang Tillmans

Interviews were conducted between 2018 and 2021, many on an ongoing basis. They have been edited and condensed for clarity.

Copy Editing
Olivia Parkes

Translation
Kennedy-Unglaub Translations,
Isabel Parkes

Lithography
hausstaetter herstellung, Berlin

Production Management
DISTANZ Verlag

Typeface
HAL Timezone

Printing and Binding
medialis Offsetdruck GmbH, Berlin

Distribution
Edel Germany GmbH
www.edel.com
international-books@edel.com

ISBN 978-3-95476-433-4
Printed in Germany

Published by
DISTANZ Verlag
www.distanz.de

With generous support from the Schenkung Sammlung Hoffmann, Staatliche Kunstsammlungen Dresden

Acknowledgements
My early readers and advocates: Dr. Dorothée Brill, Florian Fischer, and Jakob Rava. My last-minute lifeguards: Elke Giffeler and Tom Mader. My family throughout: Jacob, Olivia, Marta, Chris, Wendy, and Bart. Thank you to all the artists for your trust, and to your amazing studio teams, for such rigor and insight. Thank you, Erika.

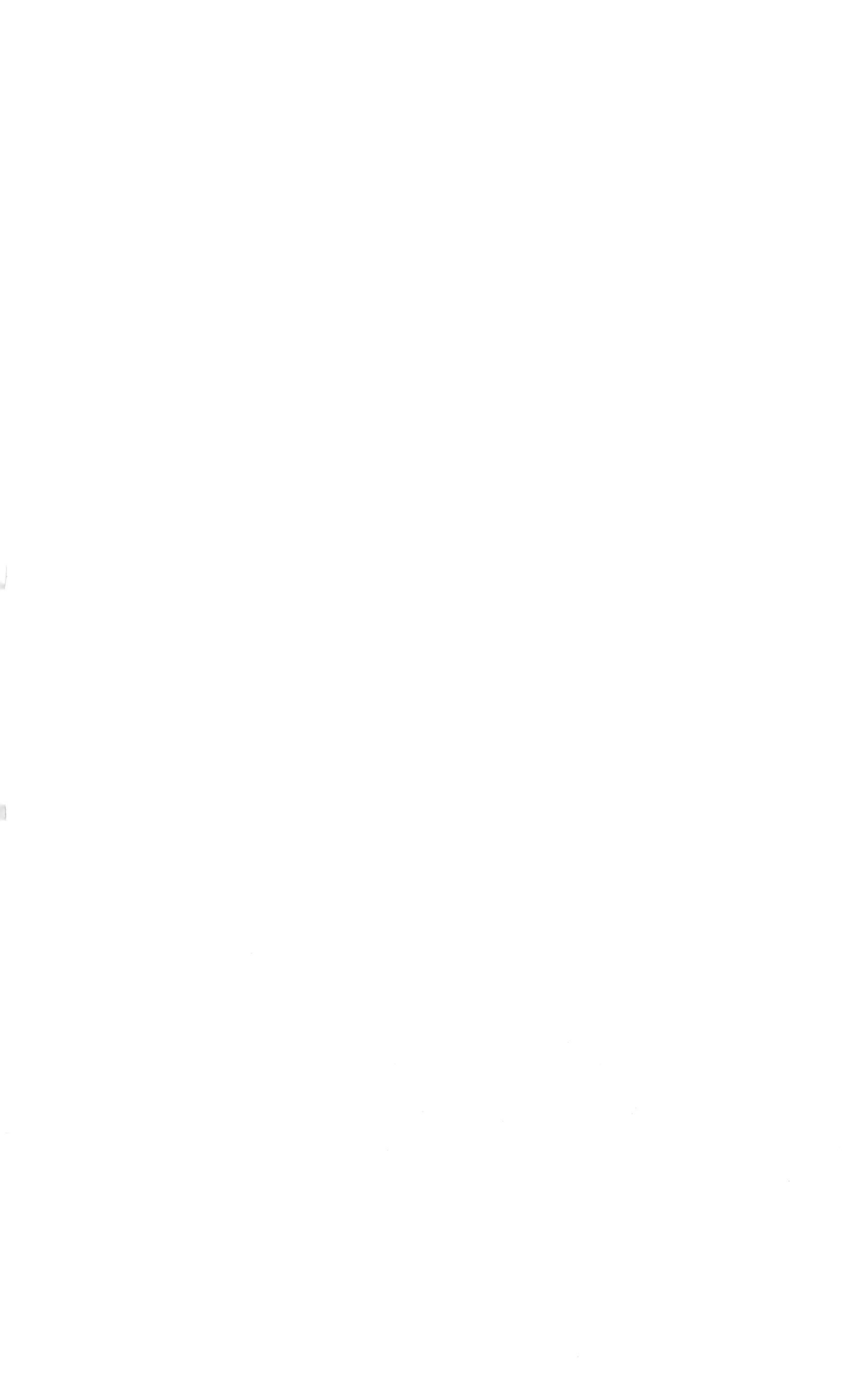